SUCCESSFUL STRATEGY EXECUTION

MICHEL SYRETT has been writing about management issues for 30 years. His work has been published in the *Sunday Times*, the *Times*, the *Financial Times*, the *Independent*, *The European*, *Management Today*, *Director*, *Asian Business* and the *South China Morning Post*. As a visiting fellow at Cranfield School of Management, the University of Hong Kong and Roffey Park Institute, he has undertaken academic research on leadership, innovation management and international human resource management.

Among the books and reports on business-related topics he has written or co-written are two Economist books on management development and innovation. He is currently researching and writing books on managing uncertainty and talent management.

OTHER ECONOMIST BOOKS

Guide to Analysing Companies
Guide to Business Modelling
Guide to Business Planning
Guide to Cash Management
Guide to Economic Indicators
Guide to the European Union
Guide to Financial Management
Guide to Financial Markets
Guide to Hedge Funds
Guide to Investment Strategy
Guide to Management Ideas and Gurus
Guide to Managing Growth
Guide to Organisation Design
Guide to Project Management
Guide to Supply Chain Management
Numbers Guide
Style Guide

Book of Isms
Book of Obituaries
Brands and Branding
Business Consulting
Business Strategy
Buying Professional Services
The City
Coaching and Mentoring
Doing Business in China
Economics
Emerging Markets
Marketing
Megachange
Modern Warfare, Intelligence and Deterrence
Organisation Culture
The World of Business

Directors: an A–Z Guide
Economics: an A–Z Guide
Investment: an A–Z Guide
Negotiation: an A–Z Guide

Pocket World in Figures

SUCCESSFUL STRATEGY EXECUTION

How to keep your business goals on target

Michel Syrett

THE ECONOMIST IN ASSOCIATION WITH
PROFILE BOOKS LTD

Published by Profile Books Ltd
3A Exmouth House, Pine Street, London EC1R OJH
www.profilebooks.com

Typeset in EcoType by MacGuru Ltd
info@macguru.org.uk

Printed in Great Britain by
Clays, Bungay, Suffolk

A CIP catalogue record for this book is available
from the British Library

Hardback ISBN 978 1 86197 894 3
Paperback ISBN 978 1 84668 605 4
ebook ISBN 978 1 84765 033 7

The paper this book is printed on is certified by the © 1996 Forest Stewardship
Council A.C. (FSC). It is ancient-forest friendly. The printer holds FSC chain of custody

FSC
Mixed Sources
Product group from well-managed
forests and other controlled sources

Cert no. SGS-COC-2061
www.fsc.org
© 1996 Forest Stewardship Council

SGS-COC-2061

Contents

Acknowledgements

First and foremost I wish to thank my dear departed friend Carol Kennedy, who died of cancer in early 2007 and to whom this book is dedicated. She was an inspiration to me and many others. Heartfelt thanks also to Damian McKinney, the founder and managing director of McKinney Rogers, who supported the research and provided the introduction to many of the organisations that agreed to be case studies. He was a constant source of encouragement and help – as were others in the firm, most notably Alan Edwards, Krissi Collett, Steven Lee, Ayako Morioka, Fred Tresler, Russ Thornton and Steve Wilson.

Thanks to the academic researchers and consultants who kindly allowed me to reproduce their work in the book. These include Lynda Gratton and Julian Birkinshaw, professors at London Business School; Kit (Catherine) Jackson of Palladium, a consultancy founded by the inventors of the balanced scorecard, Robert Kaplan and David Norton; and Karen Stephenson, president of Netform, with whom I had great fun putting together the original material that she volunteered. Thanks, Karen!

I am indebted to the senior managers who helped me research the original case studies that form the basis of the book. In particular, my thanks go to Peter Aldridge, chief executive of HSBC Rail (UK); Julian Burzynski, general manager of Judge & Dolph; Sarah Dunn, European vice-president, human resources, at Thomson Financial (now part of Reuters); H. Jin Iwamoto, chief executive of MHD (Diageo Möet Hennessy Japan); Gerald Mahinda, managing director of East African Breweries; Klaus D. Mittorp, managing director, HR communications and quality, at Deutsche Bank; John Reid-Dodick, global head of human resources for business divisions at Reuters; John Rhodes, chief executive of Luxfer Gas Cylinders; David Roblin, head of clinical R&D at Pfizer; Margaret Savage, director of HR strategic policy at British Telecom; and Bill Simon, vice-president, heath and wellness products, at Wal-Mart.

On the editorial side, thanks to Stephen Brough, Ron Emler and Penny Williams. Lastly, I would like to thank my partner Suzy for putting up with long weekends of me being chained to the computer and – good sportswoman that she is – providing essential wing support.

Michel Syrett

Preface

The basic message of this book – that successful strategy execution is about clarity of purpose, good communication, strictly controlled resource allocation, breaking strategy down into easily achieved objectives and fostering a risk-friendly culture that encourages freedom of action if it supports key strategic goals – is as true today as it was when this book was researched and originally published.

However, the context in which these actions are practised could not be more different. When the 2008 crash occurred, a year after first publication, many senior executives assumed that it was another turn in the boom-and-bust cycle that characterised macroeconomics in Western economies since the end of the second world war. They reacted accordingly, cutting costs and "hunkering down" for what they supposed would be a painful but short period of austerity.

In fact, the crash has ushered in a period of unprecedented uncertainty, with the economic unknowns added to by political and social unknowns arising from such developments as the Arab spring and the anti-capitalist and anti-austerity protests in a number of Western countries.

Uncertainty is here to stay. Not for nothing did the secretary general of the United Nations recently comment that the first years of the 21st century may well prove "a decisive moment in the human story", requiring co-operation by politicians and business leaders across all boundaries to respond to the interconnected threats the world currently faces.

From a business perspective, a more chaotic environment underlines rather than dissipates the messages outlined in this book. Uncertainty breeds fear and fear breeds paralysis – a further source of the "friction" that disrupts the effective execution of what seems a perfectly defined strategy (see Chapter 2).

As well as the focus and clarity the book advocates as a response, business leaders now have the additional task of instilling confidence and context. As Daniel Galvao, chief commercial officer at Marsh, an insurance broker and risk adviser, told the author in 2011:

> *Employees and management need to believe that there is strong leadership so that their products and services will survive at*

a time when the company may be struggling. It is a matter of instilling strong faith in the future.

Angela Casini, learning and development manager at Selex Galileo, an Italian electronics company, adds:

To step into an uncertain future, managers need confidence and especially a sense of optimism. They have to believe they can make a difference; that they can help build a positive picture of the future. If they can't do this, if they can only be negative about the future, a sense of helplessness and paralysis sinks in. The business begins to feel it is a victim and that it cannot do anything positive to shape its future.

Research conducted by the author with PA Consulting Group in 2011 has also confirmed that in the opinion of the senior executives whose views were canvassed, how strategy is determined can no longer be separated from how it is implemented because of the speed which is necessary to exploit opportunities and respond to threats in an uncertain environment.

The methods used by companies such as Luxfer Gas Cylinders and HSBC Rail profiled in this book – for example, developing strategy maps that measure progress not so much by the fulfilment of financial goals but by cross-disciplinary collaboration resulting in innovative products, services and management methods – are precisely what trendsetters in industry are now advocating on a broader scale.

Rainer Feurer, senior vice-president for corporate strategy and planning at BMW Group, for example, argues that strategy must be treated as part of individual responsibilities throughout the organisation as opposed to a central function, and that the quality of a formulated strategy depends on the quality of knowledge used.

This in turn hinges on how effectively the process of gaining knowledge is managed in the organisation. According to Feurer, strategy formulation must therefore be regarded as a constant learning process and the quality of strategy depends on the quality of the organisation's cognitive and behavioural learning mechanisms – exactly what this book advocates in Chapter 10.

Lastly, the use of techniques such as "mission leadership", highlighted in Chapter 7 as a means of creating a risk-free culture that encourages freedom of action if it supports key strategic goals, has gained significantly more credence in the years since the book was first published in 2007.

In the PA survey referred to earlier, the senior executives interviewed stressed again and again that staff empowerment of this kind was essential to successful strategy execution in an era of uncertainty. "I feel my job as a leader has always been to set the goal and then get out of the way," says one senior executive. Another adds:

> *Whatever actions the company takes, we always try to encourage a bottom-up approach which allows staff to influence the decisions. Getting the employees on the same plain as senior management has been a priority, particularly in terms of pinpointing what was happening in the external world.*

The business environment may have changed dramatically in the past few years but speed of execution, agility, effective delegation and clarity of purpose remain just as important to commercial survival and success. Indeed, in an uncertain world, they have acquired even greater relevance.

Michel Syrett
January 2012

1 Setting the scene

Vision is nothing without execution.

Mark Hurd, chief executive, Hewlett-Packard

The problem defined: vision is nothing without execution

Mark Hurd, former chief executive of Hewlett-Packard, an information technology giant, is a strange, almost incongruous, business hero. With his prim-and-proper manner and crisply knotted ties, his hair cropped short with every strand in place and his work-his-way-up-the-ladder career with National Cash Register before he joined Hewlett-Packard and then Oracle, he hardly conforms to the devil-may-care image of the modern entrepreneur.

What he did to revive the fortunes of the legendary Silicon Valley firm hardly breaks new conceptual ground either. He cut costs (and 10% of the workforce), focused the company's strategy on a few core areas and separated product divisions. He also hired senior managers from outside the famously insular company. These are the sort of routine measures that rarely generate headlines.

That, according to Hurd, is how it should be. Workaday, stick-to-basics, get-the-essentials-right management is what he thinks most companies need. As he told The Economist:[1]

> Vision without execution is nothing. Whenever anyone asks me about vision, I get very nervous. You've got to be able to tie it back to strategy; you've got to tie accountability to things.

"Vision is nothing without execution" is the best summary of this book. The implication of numerous presentations and business books is that the design and execution of strategy are a mystery that only business gurus, highly paid consultants and MBA graduates from the best business schools can unravel.

That is nonsense. Developing good business direction is not magic. Nor does it require the IQ of an Einstein. It is a tough and sometimes exhausting process that can only really be understood in the context of what a particular chief executive or senior director was trying to achieve at the time.

Effective business strategies have an almost mundane quality, usually consisting of ideas that are already known. What really matters is making sure that these ideas are right for the organisation and, more importantly, getting the rest of the organisation to agree with you.

Looking back: British Airways

Is this something new? Hardly. It was the case 25 years ago with one of the most spectacular corporate turnarounds in the 1980s, that of British Airways (BA). The vision Sir John King (later Lord King of Wartnaby) had for BA when he was appointed chairman in 1981 – "to be the world's favourite airline" – is hardly something that needed the foresight of Leonardo da Vinci. The method by which King proposed BA should achieve the goal – putting the customer first – is so blindingly self-evident that an undergraduate from any second-tier business school could have come up with it.

The trick, from King's point of view, was persuading the managers and employees at BA that he meant it. King had one focus for change that he was able to use to his advantage – the imminent privatisation of BA under a new Conservative government. This gave him a window of opportunity. It imposed an external driver that was evident to everyone, and he used it to impose several important reforms that would have been difficult to achieve in other circumstances.

Costs were savagely reduced between 1981 and 1983. Heavy financial losses in 1980 gave King the licence to remove 50 of the airline's 150 senior managers, sending a loud and clear signal to everyone that things had to change.

Firing people and cutting budgets are always the easy part. But King also used BA's message of strategic intent – put the customer first – as the focus for organisation-wide customer service campaigns, led by project teams that acted as agents of change.

This was followed in 1985 by a new marketing drive, spearheaded by initiatives to revamp the corporate image, including a new livery and new advertising campaigns. The timing of this decision was important. King waited until the internal revolution was yielding results before he started to make claims that might otherwise have been shown to be a sham once customers compared the image they saw in the advertisements with their actual experiences.

A good illustration of how difficult it is to make good strategy stick is that the revolution King initiated at BA in the 1980s has not been long-lasting and at the time of writing the company's competitive and public relations standing was at a new low.

Looking back: General Electric

At the same time, in the United States, Jack Welch, General Electric's now legendary chief executive, was turning around the multifaceted business using similarly simple tenets to those employed by King at British Airways. He took the view that if a business is not first or second in its market, you close it, sell it or fix it. Emphasise ownership, teamwork and enterprise in everything you do. Draw on and share good practice wherever you find it. Break down all internal barriers to action and communication. Become a "boundaryless" organisation, shifting resources and expertise to wherever they are most needed.

Using this philosophy, over ten years Welch transformed a company with a declining market share in every sector in which it competed into a corporate giant ranked number one in the US *Forbes* 500 throughout the early 1990s.

Looking at the present: Domaine Chandon

Between them, King and Welch created a template for strategy execution that became business school gospel and still determines the actions of chief executives today. There is little difference between the strategy adopted by Hurd at Hewlett-Packard and that adopted at General Electric 20 years ago. It is based on:

- cutting costs and unnecessary spending;
- breaking down internal barriers;
- focusing all resources on the main strategic goal;
- motivating and empowering the workforce to achieve this goal;
- boosting performance as a result.

However, in most companies this strategy does not always work. The problems Frédéric Cumenal faced when he became chief executive of Domaine Chandon in late 2001 are typical of those confronting a manager who wants to get things done but cannot.

Based in California, the company is owned by Möet Hennessy, the drinks arm of LVMH, a luxury food and drinks conglomerate. Like many champagne companies, Domaine Chandon had enjoyed buoyant demand in the run-up to the millennium. But demand, which was already faltering, slumped after the terrorist attacks on New York and Washington on September 11th 2001.

Cumenal found the company ill-equipped to adapt to the new realities of the American market. Costs were high, inefficiencies abounded, morale was low and no one was in a mood to celebrate.

The strategic solution to the transformed market was, Cumenal said, "conceptual child's play". Domaine Chandon had to focus its marketing away from sales to wine bars and restaurants towards sales through supermarkets and liquor shops.

Getting the company focused and reorganised around that strategy was another matter. Cumenal was able to revitalise his senior management team using the new strategy as an incentive, but old-fashioned objective setting did not work at other levels.

Domaine Chandon's sales teams were locked in to marketing to restaurants and wine bars. The development of an alternative marketing approach took half a year to create and months more to implement. Lack of effective delegation meant that too many decisions were passed back up to the senior management team, often to Cumenal himself. Morale remained low and performance stagnated.

A solution finally evolved (see Chapter 3). Meanwhile, Cumenal was frustrated and blocked in every direction. "We had the strategy right," he concluded. "It just didn't hang together."

Looking at the present: the case examples in this book

Cumenal's experiences are mirrored in the stories of other organisations discussed in this book (see Table 1.1). All have visions that are remarkably similar and consistent. They are to:

- be first (or a leader) in their chosen markets;
- produce a significant return on capital – either through growing organically or through acquisitions and/or by reducing costs or making more efficient use of their resources;
- be innovative and creative in their product development, service design and delivery and work practices;
- be ethical, socially aware and environmentally responsible in conducting their business.

Yet the strategies they adopted to bring about these simple visions – usually a combination of those championed in the 1980s by companies such as British Airways and General Electric – proved hard to implement and even harder to sustain.

Why? The best generic term for the collective drag on strategy is a military one: friction.

Table 1.1 **Vision and strategies**

Company/ organisation	Vision/mission	Strategy
British Airways	To be the world's favourite airline	Marketing drive to put the customer first, supported by internal training and employee communications and revamping the corporate image
General Electric	To be first or second in all chosen markets	If a business is not first or second in its market, close it, sell or fix it. Emphasise ownership, teamwork and enterprise in everything you do. Share good practice. Break down all internal barriers to action and communication. Become a "boundaryless" organisation, shifting resources and expertise to wherever they are most needed
Diageo (Asia)	To be the fastest and most entrepreneurial company in Greater Asia by 2010	Emphasis on understanding the competition, supported by internal training programmes and mission leadership conducted with staff and suppliers (see Chapter 3)
East African Breweries	To become East Africa's number one brewer by market and segment by 2010	Emphasis on innovation and unrestrained thinking, supported by mission leadership (see Chapter 3) and well-thought-out performance measures (see Chapter 9)
HSBC Rail (UK) (leasing company)	To make more efficient use of expertise and capital – and strive for improved returns on equity – by delivering a broader range of products and services	Emphasis on efficient use of funds, customer relationship management, operational excellence and learning, supported by cross-disciplinary goals such as "developing a responsive organisation that is light on its feet" (see Chapter 6)
Judge & Dolph	To move from maintaining the company's position as Illinois's leading drinks distributor to winning first place in the league of drinks distributors of the United States as a whole	To deliver a step change in business performance in the United States by becoming a "$1 billion company" by turnover to "win the war on visibility" (a goal linked to the company's need to distinguish itself from its competitors – see Chapter 6)

Company/ organisation	Vision/mission	Strategy
Luxfer Gas Cylinders	To shift the profit base from high-volume, low-margin products to customer-focused, value-added products	Developing cross-functional "themes'" covering customer focus, innovation, learning and growth, being market-led and operational excellence. At every strategic review, senior managers appointed to oversee the inculcation of these themes across the company's operations report back on progress using a series of specialist measures designed for the task (see Chapter 3)
Diageo Möet Hennessy Japan	To become the best builder of drinks brands in Asia	Using mission leadership, supported by total quality management-style coaching, to inculcate the message "We are brand-builders" throughout the workforce (see Chapter 4)
Reuters	To take "a great leap forward" in terms of the benefits of scale and business autonomy	A four-year change management programme called Fast Forward, stressing four "values" – being "fast" (working with passion, urgency, discipline and focus); accountable; service-driven; and team-spirited (see Chapter 4) – and a follow-up programme called Core Plus emphasising the need to develop new sources of revenue (see Chapter 8)
Royal National Orthopaedic Hospital	To launch a programme of clinical innovation supporting a £20m refurbishment of the main hospital campus	The creation of mutually supporting creative team roles that link the tasks of specialist medical consultants and professional hospital trust managers (see Chapter 9)
Thomson Financial (before the merger with Reuters)	To dominate its chosen field through effective differentiation	Developing new products such as the technological tool Thomson ONE, which enables its clients to tailor and use more effectively the vast array of financial data, analytical information, research, calculations and news available on its database. Supporting these kinds of products requires operational excellence and a performance culture among staff at all levels (see Chapter 6)

2 Friction

No plan survives the first two minutes of battle.

Helmuth Von Moltke, the Elder, Chief of the Imperial German General Staff, 1858–88

General Electric: turning slogans into mantras in 1990s Hungary

Jack Welch's concept of a "boundaryless" organisation was highly successful when he introduced it to General Electric's US operations in the 1980s, but it proved frustratingly difficult to export a decade later.

Local cultures and economic traditions intervened at every level. A good example is the teething pains GE encountered when it tried to introduce its business philosophy into its Hungarian subsidiary, Tungsram, following the collapse of communism between 1989 and 1991. There were predictable run-ins with the local trade unions about the job cuts totalling half the workforce that GE wanted to impose. By the early 1990s American and British unions may have been used to proposals to "downsize" the workforce; to the Hungarian unions, however, it was seen as a gross betrayal of what they had been promised when GE bought a controlling share of the company. The leader of Tungsram's independent trade union said:

> When GE acquired a majority share of the company in 1990 it was hailed by them and the Hungarian government as a shining example of how capitalist prosperity could be brought to post-communist central Europe. But at the time GE assumed full ownership of the company in 1993, much of the lustre faded in the wake of the job cuts. Tungsram's workers consequently felt betrayed by the American management.

Senior American managers went into the deal promising too much and failed to manage expectations effectively. The result was sullen and discordant industrial relations that cast a shadow over the early necessary reforms the company made to its operational processes. However, the negative impact of this early misjudgment was short-lived as the company bounced back later in the decade.

More subtle and deep-rooted were the cultural adjustments the remaining workers had to make in the wake of Welch's policies of lean, "boundaryless" cross-disciplinary working. Project manager Tibor Friucsan, who saw Tungsram's layers of management cut from 11 to three in as many months, agreed:[1]

> Our world totally changed. People who were used to a
> hierarchical structure where the boss gave the orders had to
> adjust in a very short time to the idea that decisions were taken
> by teams and not individuals.

Other problems stemmed directly from the ideological legacy of the communist era. Under a socialist system, everyone just focused on meeting the production targets that had been set (or fiddled results to make it appear they had). There was no intelligent management discipline aimed at providing what customers wanted, when they wanted (or needed) it. The result was that while GE managers regarded "Welch-speak", such as the need for managers to "release floods of ideas" and unlock "a culture of winning", as articles of faith, to workers on the factory floor they seemed confusingly similar to the propaganda of the old order about working harder and improving efficiency. They were seen as just another way of increasing responsibility and the individual workload for little extra reward.

Pfizer: dealing with discordancy

The malaise caused by the gulf in perception is understandable given the different economic and social time warps that General Electric and Tungsram inhabited in the early 1990s. But it remains enduringly familiar in 21st century companies.

In the early 2000s, Pfizer's global research and development headquarters at Sandwich in the UK was suffering from what senior line managers acknowledge was a culture of deep cynicism. Projects worth millions of dollars a day to the corporation were months late and collaborative dynamics underpinning the work of the teams was, in the words of David Roblin, vice-president of Pfizer global R&D, "discordant and reactive".

At the heart of the problem was a disconnection between the goals and activities of the scientists and technical staff working on the many clinical research projects at Sandwich, the senior "heads of lines" to whom they reported and the support functions they turned to for the resources to conduct their work.

The problem was not one of structure or operational procedure. Pfizer operates a cross-functional structure well suited to running and supporting long-term research projects and its success in developing new medicines is clear. It is also justifiably proud of its portfolio of standard operating procedures, developed over decades to facilitate and support the work of complex multidisciplinary research work.

The difficulty was that, in the eyes of many of the scientists and technicians, the system was too rigid in its application. A common complaint, for example, was that whenever a new operating procedure was introduced, technical or research staff would be pulled away from their work to undertake a two-day familiarisation and training course even if the specific procedure was not immediately relevant to the project in hand. Yet when the same staff wanted additional resources to solve immediate problems on the project – for instance, funds to attend a crucial meeting in another country – the system sometimes just did not deliver them. As one person put it:

> Consideration of our needs was seen as being driven by supply, not demand. The larger organisation was seen as thwarting, not facilitating, our work. In some camps there had developed a classic "us" and "them" mentality. The perception that the organisation would not respond to legitimate requests for support and additional resources to help cut corners or save valuable time resulted in few people testing the system at all.

Friction: the military provenance

The operational difficulties encountered by General Electric a decade ago and by Pfizer more recently have little to do with the concept of business they champion or the more immediate strategies they have adopted. They are more to do with the muddle senior managers encounter if they do not keep a grip on how the strategy is interpreted or executed two or three rungs further down the organisational ladder – a muddle best described as "friction".

Friction is a military term first articulated by the breed of 19th-century staff officers that emerged in the wake of the Napoleonic wars. It describes what goes wrong once an elaborate strategy that requires the co-ordination and collaboration of a large body of different units hits the reality of operations on the ground.

A strategy – at that time and since – derails for a number of reasons:

◪ The orders from headquarters never arrive: the message gets lost or the messenger is killed. For example, during the American civil war, the strategy for a confederate invasion of Pennsylvania was found by enemy soldiers wrapped around three cigars in a hastily abandoned campsite.

◪ The orders are discovered or decoded by the enemy. For example, the Battle of Midway and other Allied victories during the second world war were won because the enemy codes were deciphered.

◪ The orders are not clear or are misinterpreted. For example, look at what happened to the Light Brigade at the Battle of Balaclava when a poorly drafted order for a sensible flanking movement was mistaken by the local commander as a demand for a futile frontal charge.

◪ Changing or poorly perceived circumstances on the ground make the order incapable of being executed. For example, the Somme.

◪ The local commander lacks the resources to carry out the order. For example, the Somme.

◪ The local commander disagrees with the order and chooses not to execute it, as Admiral Nelson famously did when he wilfully disobeyed his superior officer's order to disengage from the enemy at the Battle of Copenhagen by "turning a blind eye" to the circumstances that prompted the order.

◪ The troops refuse to obey the order or mutiny, as happened in the French and Russian armies in 1917.

◪ The strategy is based on a false assumption. For example, the 2003 invasion of Iraq by American and British forces was based on the premise that the Iraqis would welcome the "liberators" and not revert to the long-standing but suppressed factional hostility between the minority Sunnis (of whom Saddam Hussein was the most famous) and the majority Shias.

Friction: the business version

Most of those military circumstances mirror business realities. Translated a little freely, these include the following:

◪ The target audience for the strategy is not static. For example, the staff turnover of a large organisation can be equivalent to the working population of a small town during a five-year programme of change.

◪ The goalposts change. For example, politics (big and small), egos, personalities, misunderstood intentions, turf wars, thinking in departmental terms (sometimes called "silo thinking") and changing organisational circumstances all combine to alter priorities and push the strategy down blind alleys.

◪ Poor operational accountability is rife. Either the goals do not reflect the mission or people are not held accountable for them.

◪ Necessary information is imperfect. It is not available or it is not clear or it is processed and interpreted differently by different people.

◪ Middle managers complicate things. The better-educated the individuals are, the worse the problem can become because of their ability to rationalise their reactions.

Research paints a more detailed picture of what goes wrong. A 2003 survey by the Economist Intelligence Unit, in collaboration with Marakon Associates, an international strategy consulting firm, suggests that on average companies deliver only 63% of the potential financial perform-ance their strategies promise.[2]

Even worse, the survey found, the causes of this strategy-to-perform-ance gap are all but invisible to senior management. As Michael Marakon, Marakon's managing partner, comments:

Leaders pull the wrong levers in their attempts to turn around performance – pressing for better execution when they actually need a better strategy, or opting to change direction when they really should focus the organisation on execution. The result is wasted energy, lost time and continued underperformance.

In one of the (unnamed) companies surveyed, the leadership team at a major manufacturer spent months developing a new strategy for its European business. Over the preceding half-decade six new competitors had entered the market, each using the latest in low-cost manufacturing technology and cutting prices to gain market share. The performance of the European unit – once the crown jewel of the company's portfolio – had deteriorated to the point where senior management was seriously considering selling it.

To turn round the operation, the European unit's leadership team had recommended a bold new "solutions strategy" that would capi-talise on the company's existing position to fuel growth in after-sales servicing and equipment financing. The financial forecasts were exciting

– the strategy promised to restore industry-leading returns and growth. Impressed, senior management quickly approved the plan, agreeing to provide the unit with all the resources it needed to make the turnaround a reality.

The strategy did not deliver its promise. By early 2005 the unit's performance was nowhere near what its management team had projected. Returns, while better than before, remained well below the company's cost of capital. The revenues and profits managers had expected from services and financing had not materialised and the business's costs remained much higher than those of its main competitors.

At the conclusion of the review of the strategy that resulted, the unit's general manager was adamant that the course was correct. She declared:

> It's all about execution. The strategy we're pursuing is the right one. We're just not delivering the numbers. All we need to do is work harder and smarter.

Her boss, the parent company's chief executive, was not so sure. He left the meeting unconvinced that the business would ever deliver the performance its managers had forecast.

Strategy: the make-or-break role of the line

Research undertaken by Joseph Bower and Clark Gilbert, published in *Harvard Business Review* in February 2007, goes a stage further in pinpointing the extent to which a strategy's execution – as opposed to its design – determines its success.[3]

What they found, in one study after another, is that how business really gets done has little to do with the strategy developed at corporate headquarters. Rather strategy is crafted, step by step, as managers at all levels of a company – be it a small firm or a multinational – commit resources to policies, programmes, people and facilities. Because of this, the authors argue, senior managers might consider focusing less attention on thinking through the company's formal strategy and more on the processes by which the company allocates resources.

Bower and Gilbert illustrate their conclusions with another tale of eastern Europe at the time the Berlin Wall came down. It involves Lou Hughes, who became chairman of the executive board of Opel, General Motors' European subsidiary, in April 1989. When the wall came down seven months later, Volkswagen – Germany's leading carmaker – announced a deal with East Germany's state automotive directorate to use that country's automotive manufacturing capacity and to introduce an East German car in 1994.

Had a potential response from GM been worked through at headquarters using the conventional strategy decision-making process, it would have taken a year, especially since little concrete data were available on the East German market, and East Germany remained a sovereign country with its own laws and currency and was guarded by 400,000 Soviet soldiers. Instead, Hughes – acting on the tenets of the existing GM overseas strategy, which was to make cars in large focused factories in low-wage countries – worked vigorously to secure an immediate place for Opel in the East German market without waiting for approval from GM's corporate planners.

Acting on an introduction from an Opel union member to the management team of one of the directorate's factories, Hughes negotiated, on his own authority, the right to build new capacity in East Germany. He then allowed the local factory leader to publicise the deal, induced West Germany's chancellor, Helmut Kohl, to subsidise the new plant, and drew on talents from other operating divisions of GM to make sure the facility would be state-of-the-art. GM Europe and corporate headquarters were kept informed, but local decisions drove a steady series of commitments. Thus the slower moving processes of corporate headquarters were effectively pre-empted by local management doing what it thought best for the corporation. Hughes later became GM's international operations president – a suitable reward for his initiative at Opel.

From friction to focus

From this we learn that the everyday decisions of managers two or three layers down create – or destroy – a company's strategy. However, if every member of staff is clear about what they have to achieve, they can be left free to decide how they undertake the task. For everyone to profit from this freedom, however, they must be given the right focus.

3 Focus

Business goals are often complex – but they must be simply articulated.
Damian McKinney, founder, McKinney Rogers

Luxfer Gas Cylinders: moving beyond operational excellence

In 2002, John Rhodes, chief executive (now president) of Luxfer Gas Cylinders (LGC), faced a familiar problem. The company, which makes specialist cylinders ranging from firefighters' breathing apparatus to scuba tanks and medical equipment, was one of a dozen businesses bought in 1996 from Alcan by the Luxfer Group, with the intention of turning them round and reselling them at a profit.

Rhodes had done a good job in raising the company's profitability and generating cash for the owner. He had reduced working capital, cut lead times and improved operational efficiency. Similar reforms in a number of the other former Alcan subsidiaries had enabled Luxfer to sell them on at a significantly profit.

However, LGC remained in the group and Rhodes thought: "What next?" As he explains:

> We were very production-driven and hadn't spent enough time looking outward. Operational excellence can take you only so far. You do get a bang for your buck – but it's very inward looking. If you concentrate inwardly but not outwardly, even with the most efficient, most tightly run company, the marketplace can overtake you. History is littered with examples of this.

A further issue Rhodes faced was that as the company had grown throughout its North American, European and Asian markets, a culture of regionalism had crept in. Classic business feudalism, particularly among the European managers, was creating an "us and them" mentality with the rest of the company. Rhodes concludes:

> I felt we needed to redirect where we were going, that we needed to create a strategic focus that would get everyone reading from the same page and also enable me to get the right people in place.

Focus is what Rhodes set out to provide. He brought together for a week 20 managers to draw up a roadmap that would provide a strategic route for the business, boosting the profits the company made from innovative, customer-focused breakthroughs in cylinder-making without damaging the bread–and-butter revenue it made from its existing "commoditised" products. It became the bible for the company's growth. Whenever an initiative is proposed, Rhodes is renowned for taking out his strategic roadmap, placing it on the table and asking participants to identify precisely which strategic objective their proposal supports. He uses the same tactic whenever a meeting strays from the strategic track.

To counter the embedded culture of regionalism and to further support the new strategy, Rhodes developed a series of "themes" that would underpin the operations of LGC's divisions and cut across traditional geographical and functional boundaries. These themes covered customer focus, innovation, learning and growth, being market-led and operational excellence. At every strategic review, senior managers appointed to oversee the inculcation of these themes across all the company's operations reported progress using a series of specially designed measures.

Rhodes, a psychologist by background, designed these measures not just to plot progress but also to generate discussion and engagement. He says:

> At LGC, we take considerable time to craft objective statements
> on the map so that they are powerful, relevant and meaningful.
> We define each objective in detail and agree on a set of "do
> wells" (what does "doing well" look like?) that describe the
> actions, behaviours and results expected from delivering each
> objective. This, in turn, generates considerable discussion about
> how best to implement the strategy in practical terms. The
> process drives strong consensus around the agreed priorities
> and expectations and makes the strategy understandable and
> personally relevant to those who have to execute it.

The results speak for themselves. Before 2002, 60% of LGC's profits came from manufacturing high-volume, low-margin products. By 2005, more than 60% of the profits came from new products that have often broken new ground in cylinder manufacture. They include a super-light breathing apparatus cylinder for firefighters that significantly reduces the weight they have to carry on their backs at a time when lives are at risk, and an extended-life cylinder, which can remain in service for up to

20 years, in contrast to the standard product, which must be discarded after 15 years. In a different field, LGC has developed and manufactured a high-duration gas delivery apparatus that is revolutionising home-based oxygen treatment for patients with breathing and lung disorders.

These products are a direct result of the change in culture brought about by the systematic application of the new themes. The cross-disciplinary contacts brought about by the innovation theme were directly responsible for the development of the firefighters' breathing apparatus. The breakthrough was the result of a close transatlantic working partnership between LGC's European marketing department, led by Veronique McKellican, who proposed the two new products, and the Luxfer US Composite Cylinder Division, under the leadership of Lonnie Smith (then engineering manager and since promoted to general manager of Luxfer Shanghai), who developed a new, stiffer form of carbon to facilitate their manufacture.

The greater priority placed on creating a dialogue with customers about their needs brought about the development of the gas delivery system for oxygen therapy at home. Close links with the British Lung Foundation and the Association Nationale du Traitement à Domicile des Insuffisants Respiratoires, strong patient groups in the UK and France respectively, helped the company's R&D department define what patients required in terms of product definition for long-term oxygen therapy at home.

These links started in 2001 and have since allowed LGC to talk directly to patients, respiratory nurses and consultants to give them a better understanding of the issues associated with home treatment of respiratory ailments. This, coupled with good contacts established with the medical divisions of most global gas companies, formed the basis of a series of brainstorming sessions in Europe and the United States to specify a product that would meet both the needs of the patients and the financial requirements of customers, in terms of financial returns and product positioning compared with existing technologies.

It was established that some European countries were already well advanced in terms of prescribing lightweight, small, portable equipment to allow patients mobility. France, Germany and Italy have an established system of calculating the payback that caters for the financial "burden" of portable liquid systems, whereas the UK, Belgium and eastern European countries usually put patients on "restrictive" concentrators or large and heavy cylinders.

Using this knowledge, LGC developed a lightweight, small, high-duration gas delivery system that would both meet the patients' portability needs and, equally as important, reduce the investment required as well as the recurring distribution and servicing costs to its first-tier customers. It produced a high-strength, alloy-lined, carbon-wrapped 300lb cylinder fitted with a lightweight valve and regulator. The system is "enclosed" in an ergonomically designed case with the added advantage of an in-built oxygen-conserving device that offers a long duration, portable alternative to the (more expensive) liquid systems.

Rhodes argues that the cross-disciplinary collaboration and in-depth dialogue with customers that underpinned both these product break-throughs would simply not have occurred in the culture that existed in the company before 2002. He says:

> *The focus on differentiating products, providing a value-added premium and getting to the market quickly was not there. There was a prevailing mindset that said: "This is my train set. I want to play with my train set. You play with yours"*

Focusing on "hot spots"

Rhodes has grasped the most important aspect of successful strategy execution: focus. The right focus gets people engaged. The early involvement of a broad cross-section of LGC's managers in determining the strategy generated a regular stream of groundbreaking projects arising directly from the priority given to innovation and customer focus.

Lynda Gratton, professor of management practice at London Business School and an expert on human resource strategy, puts it differently. She says it is about finding people's "hot spots".[1]

Hot spots = (co-operative mindset × boundary spanning × igniting purpose)

Productive capacity

A hot spot is Gratton's description of the energy that makes sure best-practice ideas are incorporated into productivity improvements. Her study of the retention and performance management strategies of 20 companies revealed that when a hot spot flares, it is through the "spontaneous combustion" of three elements:

- **A co-operative mindset.** The energy that makes up a hot spot is sparked by productive personal relationships between talented staff. As Gratton puts it, value is created in the space between people. People are excited and willing to co-operate and it is these co-operative relationships that keep them engaged. However, she continues:

> Where hot spots fail, we found that human capital rapidly atrophied. People lose interest and the intellectual challenge is gone. They withdraw emotionally as the passion of the project wanes and this is as good as losing them physically.

- **Crossing boundaries.** This is the energy that keeps individuals engaged across a company's functional and wider boundaries. These relationships enable innovation to emerge and expertise to be exploited. However, this level of co-operation will not occur spontaneously. It needs the spark of an igniting purpose.
- **An igniting purpose.** The flaring of a hot spot is always accompanied by something that people find exciting and with which they are prepared to engage. This might be in the form of a question (such as "how can we as a company become a force for good?") that awakes curiosity. Or it might take the form of a task or purpose. For example, the BBC galvanised its workforce by its coverage of the 2006 World Cup. It extended the planning and execution of the programming to as wide a range of its workforce as possible, making the event a cross-disciplinary and collaborative project that acted as a "hot spot", helping to unify the broadcaster.

Gratton's concept is based on the pioneering practice of about 20 companies with which she has worked extensively over the past five years.

At Nokia, for example, complex networks based on strong relationships and "acquaintances groups" were critical to the company's ability to update its products. Within modular product teams, software developers frequently knew each other well and were able to develop and share complex tacit knowledge. Senior managers at Nokia went to great lengths to keep the teams intact even through the company's frequent reorganisations.

Similarly, at British Petroleum, "peer" groups and "peer challenge" were crucial to knowledge sharing. Clusters of up to 13 units from around the world, grouped together roughly by market, were given the task of developing not only their own capabilities but also those of other business units within the peer group.

Domaine Chandon: from focus to clarity

Gratton is quick to point out that hot spots cannot be created by command. They arise naturally through the choice of participants, when their excitement and curiosity are engaged. She says:

> The challenge is that in many companies, we have – often unwittingly – created places where competition and self-interest negate skilful co-operation. But the good news is that much of this can be changed. We can craft the practices and processes of our companies to favour co-operation rather than competition – and keep our best talent effectively engaged in the process.

But the very serendipity that Gratton highlights raises a second priority. A common focus is not the only requirement for the effective execution of strategy: clarity is equally important. The research undertaken by Joseph Bower and Clark Gilbert, professors at Harvard Business School (see Chapter 2), suggests that decision-making in organisations spans many levels, with activities of key individuals proceeding on parallel, independent tracks.

The notion of a top-down strategic process, Bower and Gilbert argue, depends upon a central control of all steps that is rarely possible.[2] As described in Chapter 2, at the same time that headquarters staff plan for and roll out initiatives, local managers are invariably acting in ways that either undermine or enhance them. For this reason, everyone at all levels has to be clear about the purpose of the strategy, the role they play in fulfilling it and the role their colleagues and collaborators play.

Breaking strategy into easy deliverable objectives, combined with intensive team-based coaching, solved the problems faced by Frédéric Cumenal, chief executive of Domaine Chandon, highlighted in Chapter 1.

Lack of effective delegation meant that too many decisions were passed back up to the top team, in many cases to Cumenal himself. Morale was low and performance had stagnated. Cumenal adopted a technique called "Mission Leadership", which is based on the command and delegation protocols adopted by the American and British forces during the Gulf wars against Iraq. Everyone, from senior to junior managers, is trained to arrive at an analysis of the task which covers an appraisal of the situation, the guiding purpose set one or two levels above them, the implied tasks and the boundaries defining their freedom to act. The military origins of mission leadership and the concept of effective "command" as it applies to business management are outlined in the Appendix.

The key to a mission analysis is that it identifies at an early stage the "main effort" of the strategy and stops people lower down from diverting attention and activity away from it. In Domaine Chandon's case, the main effort was to focus people's attention away from sales to bars and restaurants towards sales to supermarkets and liquor stores.

The tasks of each department were broken down into easy-to-understand objectives. The senior management team briefed the managers immediately below them, a process repeated throughout the company until everybody understood what they were doing and why they were doing it.

Things started to move. The first thing Cumenal noticed was an increase in motivation and confidence, largely because once people understood what the goal was and how their own task contributed to it, they were left free to explore how to attain it. The number of e-mails he received dropped dramatically. In time each department did not need to refer to the strategy to check whether its own objectives were on track. It came naturally.

By the end of 2003, the results were "spectacular". All the numbers that mattered such as asset utilisation, cash generation and profitability had risen to historic highs. Cumenal reflects:

> We had not been using our human assets. A proper focus on the "mission" released potential. It has been a fantastic way of getting a real competitive advantage by leaving people free to explore the "how" once you are sure they properly understand the "why".

Lipper: clarity as bedrock

The back-to-basics approach of accurate objective setting, focused resource allocation and encouraging initiative around a universally understood set of goals does not depend on size.

Among the enthusiasts is Michael Peace of Lipper, a consultancy that employs just 420 staff to monitor and provide data and analysis about the mutual fund industry. When he took over in September 2001, Lipper was forecast to lose more than £5m on revenues of £24m. Three years later the company made a £5m profit on revenues of £32m.

Building on Lipper's new-found financial success, Peace also used the measures and accountability imposed by a mission leadership approach to integrate the operations of a series of smaller fund intelligence firms it acquired. These include Hardwick Stafford Wright and Bopp, and more recently Capital Access and Fitzrovia. Peace says:

A clear focus means clear job descriptions and clear ownership of the role. We have fewer role titles and a framework based on the tasks associated with a mission. For mission leadership to be effective it has to be actively transmitted via this framework. Each member of staff has a single sheet of paper showing the mission and the key deliverables, which are in a database to ensure objectivity, measurability and integrity. This clarity is the bedrock of any performance measurement and, more importantly, personal reward. Through the rhythm of a mission, we were able to develop a set of tasks with clear deliverables with owners and a reward structure based on this transparency.

Pfizer: turning around its teams

Mission leadership also helped Pfizer to overcome the cynicism it encountered among its R&D teams (see Chapter 2). It was this sense of passive resignation that David Roblin, then Pfizer's head of clinical R&D, wanted to overturn using the mission leadership concept. He recognised that cynics are often frustrated idealists and that if the significant resources and expertise of the organisation could be properly aligned with the specific needs of the project teams, and be seen to do so, the change in attitudes and behaviour could be dramatic.

Two problems in particular were high on Roblin's list to tackle. The first was the need for clarity. As he explains:

Getting people to sit down and go through the intellectual articulation of a simple mission is more problematic than it initially seems. Many people think they have done it when in fact they haven't. For example, there is no point in setting tight deadlines for a research project to have reached a certain point in the clinical or regulatory process if the purpose of the exercise is first to question whether the market wants it. That is putting the cart before the horse.

Getting this right requires the line managers to be very clear from the outset about what the mission is, and to pause sufficiently in the consultation to ensure awareness and understanding. It then requires clinical research staff on the projects to make clear the way they drew up statements of what they needed to do the job.

To achieve this, we decided to review the way we consulted and communicated. We found, for example, that the large project

> *meetings we were holding every week were good for achieving alignment between the project's main mission and the goals of the organisation but were not a good forum for detailed planning or for breaking down decisions into sub-missions.*
>
> *The various components of a large, multidisciplinary clinical research team – pharmaceutical scientists, regulatory experts, manufacturing experts – all needed to talk to each other on a regular basis. Much smaller groups were needed to achieve this.*

The second priority Roblin identified was the need for empowerment – in this case, the empowerment that would emerge when, having established a clear idea of the main mission, the staff in clinical research teams felt able to harness the resources of the rest of the organisation and explore innovative ways to keep the project on track. Roblin wanted to demonstrate to scientific and technical staff that the "system" would work for them if it were creatively challenged:

> *Often their sense that the system was working against them was based on untried and untested assumptions. I threw out a challenge to one team that if they could identify the barriers that were being placed in their path, I'd personally remove them. On investigation, they found that most of the procedures or processes they saw as obstructive were precedents set by previous teams rather than by management. In the end, the only thing they wanted that we had to change a policy on was the ability to send out for sandwiches out of hours.*

The concepts of mission leadership, outlined to Pfizer's line managers and team members, stressed the need for leadership styles based on clarity and simplicity and the role of communication and visibility, as well as an increase in individual awareness of the impact of their own behaviour and how it could be modified to improve overall effectiveness. In terms of effective execution, it stressed:

- the need for a strategic mission and goals for a team;
- group alignment with the intention behind their objectives and a clear focus for their allocation of time and resources;
- commitment to a target end-state for the business at the end of a 12-month period and individual responsibilities for achieving that with measurable outputs;

- a clear understanding of personal and collective operating space and their interdependencies.

The results can be seen clearly in the successful completion six months ahead of schedule of one of Pfizer's most important projects: the clinical research undertaken into the use of one of its main drugs, Revatio (more popularly known as Viagra) to help patients suffering from pulmonary arterial hypertension (PAH). Viagra is used to treat male impotence by controlling more effectively the flow of blood to the penis. Studies have also shown, however, that it can help control the width of the blood vessels in the lungs, increasing the distance people are able to walk, for instance, and decreasing pressure in the pulmonary artery.

The ability of Pfizer's research team successfully to register Revatio's use as a legitimate treatment for PAH was important not just because of the millions of dollars the company earned from having the drug on the market for this use ahead of time, but also because it had been used to treat PAH informally for a number of years and it was important for the treatment to be validated by formal clinical research.

The project leader, Colin Ewen, stresses the role mission leadership played in enabling the company to stress the importance of the research and its strategic intent in conducting it:

> It enabled us to establish the strategic objective clearly in people's heads in advance, reach a strategic agreement on objectives and review progress against the original plan.

But the real benefit, he stresses, mirroring Roblin's conclusions, was the freedom it granted team members to follow their own instincts and ideas in how to achieve their own objectives, so long as this supported the project's main mission:

> Previously there had been reluctance among staff to explore this freedom. There was a worry that some gung-ho project leader would place them in an awkward position that would have repercussions when their performance was reviewed and appraised at the end of the year by their heads of line. They never explored the boundaries because they did not feel they had been given the licence to.
>
> I gave them that licence. I told them that they could do

anything as long as it is not illegal, involves fraud or contravenes government regulations.

Delegation and discretionary powers: the essence of military command

Both Roblin and Ewen recognise one of the most important principles of mission leadership which stems from its original use as an integral part of American and British military command doctrine: if people have a precise idea of what they are being asked to achieve, they will feel freer to explore how they achieve it.

They attended a seminar for commercial managers organised by the UK's Ministry of Defence and were struck by the similarities between commanding a military operation and running a multidisciplinary clinical research project with complex interdependent goals between specialists working in their own area of expertise. Roblin says:

> *Having gone into the seminar with a perception that military forces always operated at a peak of efficiency, I was interested to discover that the generals and admirals we talked to had remarkably similar logistical and resource problems to our own. Like us, they are at their best in a crisis. In an emergency, when lives are at risk and minds are fully engaged, everybody pulls together. When the situation eases, things start to unravel.*
>
> *We are no different. The goal of good project management at Pfizer is therefore not to let things slip and to keep everybody in mind of what they signed up for, while at the same time having the common sense to trust professionals to get on with what they know best.*

The link with military command doctrine was also stressed by Colonel Ian Sinclair, chief of the military planning service in the UN's Department of Peacekeeping Operations, at a private dinner in New York hosted by McKinney Rogers, a consultancy specialising in the concept. It was attended by senior managers from organisations as diverse as JWT, an advertising agency, HBO, a television production company, Diageo, a global drinks company, and JP Morgan Chase, an investment bank.

Mission command, as described by Sinclair, has the following elements:

◪ A commander gives his orders in a manner that ensures his

subordinates understand his intentions, their own missions and the context of those missions.

- Subordinates are told what they are to achieve and the reason it needs to be achieved.
- Subordinates are given the resources they need to carry out their missions.
- The commander uses the minimum control measures (so as not to limit the freedom of action of subordinates).
- Subordinates then decide (within their delegated freedom) how best to achieve their mission. Put more simply: "Tell me what to do, not how to do it."

These basic command principles, Sinclair stressed, were even more important in the case of operations of the type involved in Afghanistan and Iraq. The command complexities of multilateral coalitions require the utmost clarity of intent if the conflicting needs of different priorities, reflected in UN mandates, are to be reconciled and properly interpreted by military personnel. A fuller explanation is outlined in the articles in the Appendix.

From clarity to communication

Sinclair's focus on clarity as the principal denominator of effective command is endorsed by Damian McKinney, founder of McKinney Rogers, a former marine officer who has championed the adaptation of the concept of military command to business.

Business goals, he stresses, are often complex but they must be articulated simply:

> Strategies can only be sustained by clarity of purpose and
> clarity can only be achieved through changes in behaviour ...
> The capacity for people to get the wrong end of the stick is
> never ending and constantly reinforced by poor management.
> Persistent but sensitive vigilance is needed to check false
> perceptions and over-interpretation of simple objectives.

The next piece of the strategy execution jigsaw is effective communication.

4 Communication

If you want to build an organisation that unshackles the human spirit, you're going to need some decidedly unbureaucratic management principles.

Gary Hamel, *Leading the Revolution and Competing for the Future*[1]

Diageo Möet Hennessy Japan: words really matter

Diageo, the world's biggest wines and spirits group, has good reason to be interested in mission leadership because clarity of intent is even more important in companies where the effective distribution of their products is handled by external suppliers.

Diageo's relationship with distributors is particularly important in Asia, where the company is engaged in a head-to-head battle with its global rival, Pernod Ricard, and where its "mission" – to be the fastest and most entrepreneurial company in Asia by 2010 – is inculcated into not only every one of its employees in the region but also throughout its network of suppliers.

Good communication throughout the supply chain lies at the heart of the strategy, a message not lost on H. Jin Iwamoto, chief executive of Diageo Möet Hennessy Japan, the conglomerate's main Asian distributor. He says:

> *In Japan, words are really important. Distilling your message into the right inspirational phrase using precise language is a key part of the way we motivate people. And the way this message is reinforced and translated into objectives throughout the organisation will determine whether your strategy is a success.*

When Iwamoto took over the company in 2004, his most urgent task was to enthuse a badly demotivated workforce. The joint venture with Diageo was both an asset and a source of tension. MHD people had confidence in a range of big brand products that included the Dom Perignon and Möet & Chandon champagnes, Baileys liqueur and Hennessy cognac. But successive drops in performance had destroyed confidence in their company's ability to build and exploit the brands in the region. Iwamoto explains:

It was not the strategy that was the problem, it was the people. They had a lack of confidence in the company. There was a lack of trust in local managers. The company had experienced declining performance for 14 consecutive years. Older people had failed to meet their targets for many years – but the performance bonus linked to these targets was paid anyway because nobody wanted to demotivate them further.

The most common flaw in strategy execution identified by the Economist Intelligence Unit study (see page 11) – that a consistent gap between targets and results fosters a culture of under-performance – was the problem Iwamoto had to tackle. MHD employees expected to miss their targets but this failure incurred no sanctions, so it had become the norm that performance commitments were not and could not be kept.

In a culture firmly rooted in haiku poetry and an ethos of total quality management, Japanese companies put a premium on short, pithy corporate statements of intent that act as a rallying cry and a focus for the commitment of their workers. For example, Suntory, a Japanese brewer and distiller, bases its strategy on the mission that it is a "Growing and Good Company" which continually strives to create value for its customers and stakeholders, with "good" meaning "good at what it does" and also "good for the society in which it operates". The energy and commitment of its workers are also channelled using the slogan "*Yatte Minahare*" or "Go for it!".

Iwamoto needed to create slogans for MHD that would focus his workers' attention on the specific challenges the company faced. Unlike indigenous Japanese competitors such as Suntory, Sapporo and Kirin, whose prime role was to produce and sell their own brands and which merely acted as distributors for the products of overseas companies, MHD was set up specifically to create new demand for Diageo's leading brands.

Iwamoto therefore distilled the purpose of the company into a defining statement: "Become the Best Brand Builder". The focus for the workforce – no more than 300 people – is to build the presence and equity of Diageo's brands in Asia. The second priority is to be better at it than anyone else. Because the role of marketing and distributing foreign brands is secondary in other Japanese companies, whose prime task is manufacturing and selling their own, MHD should have succeeded in reaching this goal. Before Iwamoto's appointment, it had failed dismally.

The single task of building brands provided Iwamoto with a unifying identify for the company. The goal of being better at the task than anyone else provided him with a vision for the workforce. The challenge was to translate that goal into a set of team and individual targets that would stick.

The approach enabled Iwamoto to break down the overall task – "Become the Best Brand Builder" – into measurable tasks. With Baileys, a cream liqueur then little known in Japan, the main effort was to grow the brand exponentially, summed up in the slogan "Grow Baileys". In the case of Hennessy, once the cognac market leader in Asia but now lagging behind competitors, the task was revitalising the brand. With Diageo's scotch brands, where MHD faces intense competition from local brands such as Suntory, the task was to "Beat the Competition in the Scotch Category".

Company-wide goals included "building a fighting-fit organisation", "establishing a high-performance culture" and "delivering successful value creation". Each task was undertaken by a specific team which was given targets directly related to the goal. These targets were reviewed annually and, as they progressed, quarterly. Overall, Iwamoto set the company the goal of increasing revenue growth each year by 2%.

Staff morale, and how this translated into behaviour and performance, was a particular concern for Iwamoto:

> *The challenge wasn't that people didn't understand the mission. It was that they didn't have the confidence to believe they were capable of it after decades of poor performance. So a major task for me was to find ways of enabling them to prove it to themselves. Let me stress here that it wasn't whether I believed they could do it. It was whether they believed it.*

To provide his workers with a "proving stone", Iwamoto set the company an early benchmark of success, deliberately setting the bar as high as he dared. A priority for Diageo was to increase the revenue it derived from premium brands such as Dom Perignon champagne. The market for fine wines in Japan has grown recently as more and more families entertain at home. But simply setting a target for higher sales was not Iwamoto's sole aim. He proposed increasing the retail price by 14% as a deliberate marketing challenge to the company:

> *I set the company the task of proving to the customer that the value of the brand was worth the increased price. To focus*

people's attention on the revenue target across the board, I used the analogy that just as human beings need money to live, so does a company. To do that it must grow. No company has a right to live unless it earns more.

When the projected growth target was not met after the first year, Iwamoto sent an important signal to the company by not paying the full bonus:

We awarded people only 35% of the bonus. It was a huge shock. We also introduced a new performance management framework so that decisions about bonuses in the future could be better justified and understood.

The new performance framework was underpinned by appraising how individuals were responding to the new targets. Feedback from the appraisal after two years suggested that although there was a strong increase in pride in what the company was achieving and in the energy and ideas being generated, few people were sufficiently committed to effective teamwork and the focus on customer care.

Iwamoto responded by introducing intensive team coaching to reinforce the importance he placed on team unity, expressed by the slogan "One Team, One Vision". Formal coaching was supported by company awards. At the ceremony at which these were presented, games designed to reinforce team spirit added colour and fun.

For example, "Kitchen Stadium", a popular television programme in Japan, was reproduced as a team game in which four groups competed in cooking curry. Each team was allocated a budget based on their "One Team, One Vision" performance scores and had to purchase ingredients, cook the curry and co-ordinate a table setting. The leadership team set up by the company to co-ordinate improvements in team performance then judged which team produced the best curry in terms of taste and presentation. A big tent was pitched outside the hotel to hold more than 300 people. A tower was erected in the centre of it from which the host (an MHD employee) could describe how each team was progressing. Each comprised up to 70 people who had to work together to produce the best tasting and best looking curry.

By January 2006 it was clear that Iwamoto's strategy was paying off. The company was able to announce that it had exceeded its annual growth targeted for 2005 by achieving 4.9% growth – more than double the projected growth. The increase in confidence among delegates at MHD's annual company meeting was visible.

But Iwamoto is not resting on his laurels:

> We originally set ourselves a ten-year target to turn around the company's fortunes. Now I would like to achieve it in eight or six years. We originally set ourselves the target of 2% revenue growth a year. Now I have set the target for month-on-month growth. We have succeeded in achieving this for ten consecutive months.
>
> I like to compare it to the Olympics. A successful athlete when he is a child does not know whether he wants to be a swimmer or a long-distance runner or any other kind of athlete. He just knows he wants to win a gold medal. We have reached the point where at MHD we know what kind of athlete we want to be and we have developed the skills to compete in our chosen specialism. For the past three years, we have been competing in the regional heats. Now we are competing in the national championships.

Communication or consultation: the new realities

Iwamoto is lucky to live in country where a strong total quality management tradition – with its emphasis on cascade-style corporate transformation – and a tradition of haiku verse (brief, carefully structured lines that distil a message) make it easy to rally workers around a single clear mission.

In Western companies it is not always so easy. The clarity of intent that mission leadership is designed to deliver at all levels of the organisation has been made more difficult to achieve by several newer employment trends:

- more employed people working part-time or from home;
- larger organisations cutting the number of people they employ directly;
- more "intermediate" workers being used (that is, staff employed by external suppliers on behalf of an organisation which has little or no direct control over their work but whose corporate brand is directly affected by their commitment to its goals and values).

The full extent of the change has only recently become clear with the entry of the latest generation of 18–25 year-olds to the labour market. A survey of young people by *The Economist* found that they had the following characteristics:[2]

- **They welcome change.** Young adults are by nature well-suited to the unpredictable workplace of the future. They have less baggage and can therefore afford to take risks.
- **They think differently.** Where years of education, training and experience were once necessary to succeed, the emphasis is now on high energy, fast thinking and quick learning. Being self-taught is no longer a barrier.
- **They are independent.** Today's twentysomethings came of age as the social contract between employers and workers was dissolving. They have never expected loyalty from a company, nor have they expected to give it. They define themselves by their skills, not the firm they work for. If they have reached this point, what about those entering the job market immediately behind them?
- **They are entrepreneurial.** The survey quotes Margaret Reagan, a consultant with Towers Perrin, a consultancy that studies workforce trends, who predicted in 1999 that barely one-third of young people entering the workforce in the subsequent decade would take steady jobs with companies.
- **They want opportunity more than money and security.** They would take a cut in salary or work from home on a reduced income to build up the enterprise they want and can control or influence, rather than take a well-paid job that leaves them powerless.

Further research by the author in a study of 18–25 year-olds conducted for a previous book[3] suggests that the social networks built up by most of today's young adults owe far less to mainstream corporate culture than those of their parents or elder siblings at the same age. A far higher proportion of these networks are likely to be made up of peers who are home-based free agents, who regard old-fashioned brand image-building with suspicion and whose social (as well as professional) lives do not revolve around a constant, all-encompassing workplace.

Furthermore, having been exposed to brand marketing from an early age, the new generation of workers are well aware of any form of sales proposition, including the kind encompassed by missions, values and goals connected directly to an employer's brand. They are savvy, suspicious and far fussier about what propositions they back.

IBM: test-marketing new values

Just how fussy they are was driven home to IBM in a genuinely two-way dialogue with thousands of its employees via the corporate intranet prompted by the incoming chief executive, Sam Palmisano, when he set about revamping the corporation's core values. They had to be values that people really believed in and the workforce had to feel it had a role in shaping them. Accordingly, Palmisano proposed four concepts as possible bases for the new values, but merely as a starting point for discussion:

- Respect
- Customer
- Excellence
- Innovation

These were "test-marketed" through surveys and focus groups involving more than 1,000 IBM employees. The notion of respect was thrown out because of its associations with past IBM culture. It was also decided that statements rather than single words would be more compelling. Out of this process came the three proposed values discussed during the July 2003 forum:

- Commitment to the customer
- Excellence through innovation
- Integrity that earns trust

Using a specially tailored tool – based on IBM's e-classified software but "turbocharged" to process constantly changing content – analysts distilled the millions of words that were posted into a series of coherent themes. The results indicate just how complex negotiating common values can be when a well-educated and modern-minded workforce takes them seriously.

Many people, for example, said that a departmental mentality pitted the business units against one another to the detriment of the organisation as a whole. Several characterised this as a trust issue, but the proposed value "integrity that earns trust" was criticised as being too vague. Some thought it was just another way of saying "respect for the individual", one of the original basic beliefs that many now view as outdated. The notion of trust was also seen as being too inwardly focused – management trusting its employees – and not prescriptive enough in terms of how employees should behave with each other or stakeholders outside the company.

Drawing on this analysis, as well as feedback from surveys conducted before and after the July exercise and a full reading of the raw transcripts, a small team (with input from Palmisano) arrived at a revised set of corporate values:

- ◪ Dedication to every client's success
- ◪ Innovation that matters – for our company and the world
- ◪ Trust and personal responsibility in all relationships

This was posted on the company intranet the following November.

Palmisano's assessment of the exercise provides a good starting point for any business change strategist:[4]

> You could employ all kinds of traditional, top-down management processes, but they wouldn't work at IBM – or, I would argue, at an increasing number of 21st century companies. You just can't impose command-and-control mechanisms on a large, highly professional workforce. I'm not talking about scientists, engineers and consultants. More than 200,000 of our employees have college degrees. The chief executive can't say to them: "Get in line and follow me" or "I've decided what your values are." They're too smart for that. And, you know, smarter people tend to be, well, a little more challenging – you might even say cynical.

Networks not hierarchies: the new social imperative

In this respect, networks have become as important to communication and consultation exercises connected to successful strategy execution as hierarchies. One of the important byproducts of the study and tracking of mergers and acquisitions, for example, has been the realisation of how important informal networks are in the daily lives of companies rather than the hierarchies through which formal communications are normally channelled.

Invited by the IBM Advanced Business Institute (ABI), Karen Stephenson, a corporate anthropologist, continued her research on the three principal figures in these networks who are those best able to communicate and tap the response to major strategy initiatives. These are the people who shape the conversation in the corridors, those who play a critical role in succession planning and those who decide who stays or goes during mergers or downsizing exercises.

Particularly important are the "hubs", who communicate with the most people, the "gatekeepers", who link the various parts of the business through a small number of critical relationships (the "right" people), and the "pulse-takers", whose cross-functional responsibilities cut across hierarchical divisions and whose web of relationships allows them to know what everyone in the organisation is thinking or feeling.

Gaining the support of such people, Stephenson argues, is crucial if any change or initiative is to succeed. A forward-thinking chief executive, for example, might want to test the ground before introducing or even piloting an innovative way of working. He or she would use the hubs and gatekeepers to spread news about the impending change on a semi-formal basis and then, a few days or weeks later, garner the "word on the street" from the pulse-takers. As Stephenson concludes:[5]

> A good metaphor would be to see the organisation as a high
> security room laced with laser beams and electronic eyes. An
> innocent gambol across the room will set off a series of alarms.
> If you are unaware of pre-existing alliances connecting people,
> you too can unwittingly set off cultural alarms. Therefore,
> harnessing the power of networks is the key to efficiently putting
> in place strategies that require the unreserved commitment and
> motivation of highly knowledgeable and engaged workers.

Stephenson is informal networking personified. A highly independent academic with a background in quantum chemistry and a track record of research into ancient human trading networks (who, as one leading management writer put it recently, "ploughs her own furrow"[6]), she has held professorships and lectured at UCLA, Harvard's Graduate School of Design, Massachusetts Institute of Technology's Sloan School of Management, Imperial College London and currently Rotterdam School of Management. The offices of her web consultancy, NetForm, are above a rambling second-hand bookstore in Greenwich Village in Manhattan.

Stephenson bases her approach on a specialised methodology, supported by dedicated software for analysing human networks, for which she owns the patents. She works within corporations by briefly interviewing or issuing short, confidential questionnaires to at least 80%

of the employees. Questions will include who they work with, from whom they seek advice on career issues, with whom they collaborate creatively and who they "hang about with".

With the data fed into the software, she is able to chart the different networks operating immediately below formal hierarchies that do not, in her view, reflect the realities of the latitude and attitude of modern working life.

At Hewlett-Packard, a company she considers to be totally networked, she used a form of social network analysis to help the company recover its networks from endless reorganisations in the run-up to its merger with Compaq (see Chapter 9). At Merrill Lynch, her methods were deployed to find out why some of its human resource managers were more globally effective than others. At JP Morgan, she developed a pre-merger due diligence to be used in merger and acquisition valuations. And at Steelcase, a large American office equipment manufacturer, her software was modified for designing office space for clients based on creating and sustaining "good communication flows".

Her methods are frequently used in the run-up to and immediate aftermath of mergers and acquisitions, where skilful use of gatekeepers and pulse-takers can predict likely areas of conflict or help identify and reassure the best talent. Her use of social network analysis reached a new height of application in the aftermath of the terrorist attacks in the United States on September 11th 2001. Both the American and British governments drew on, and learned from, her knowledge of hidden networks and how, she argues, they can undermine conventional security measures and traditional military responses.

Stephenson stresses that a thoughtful and deliberate social network analysis is crucial to any successful execution of strategy. As she explains:

> When organisations are cruising along, their networks are normally in a "resting pulse" – involving routine daily contacts, transactions and functional discussions. But when a major strategic initiative occurs, a number of other networks come into place that senior executives need to access in order to get their message across and keep in touch with how people in the organisation respond. There are many networks in a culture which together form a hierarchy of trust, but among the many there are a few that are most critical to mergers.
> The first is the social network – the people both inside and

outside work with whom others discuss what is going on. The second is the innovation network – people who feel they trust one another well enough to sound out new ideas on each other and perhaps challenge the status quo or accepted ways of doing things.

Next is the expert network – people who have a stored knowledge of the organisation, its legacies and to whom others turn for expertise. Then there is the career guidance network – mentors or the people to consult about one's future. Finally, there is the learning network – people who make improvements by bridging the gap between old (expert knowledge) and new (innovation).

All of these networks come into play during a major strategic initiative. Senior executives will want to use the social network to take the pulse of how people on the ground are responding to change. Strategic initiatives disturb the resting pulse of an organisation's culture and will inevitably produce a shift, signalling people to challenge the accepted ways of doing things. At this time, the innovation network will come into play.

During any time of change, people will be nervous about the impact of the change on their careers – and senior executives will want to use gatekeepers, who are nearly always part of the career guidance network, to send out the appropriate signals to the people they want to retain, advance or develop. Finally, strategic change nearly always involves some upheaval of traditional ways of working, so the expert network will be activated, sometimes resisting change as it has a vested stake in keeping things the way they are. Resolution is achieved when there is alignment between the innovation and expert networks, usually brought about by the individuals who comprise the learning network. Here the learners respect the legacy of traditional knowledge as well as understanding how innovation must be incorporated to ensure that the business can move forward.

Since September 11th 2001 there has been an increase in the use of social network analysis, so Stephenson offers this warning: anyone can connect the dots using software to produce a network map and anyone can run simple statistical analyses to produce simple answers to simple mathematical tests. What is important, she argues, is to understand how these networks merge and diverge given the organisation's maturity, the health of its culture and its capacity to absorb small or sweeping changes.

Reuters: fast forwarding corporate transformation

Reuters did not draw on Stephenson's expertise when designing and executing its "Fast Forward" change strategy – but it might well have done. The communications and consultation exercise envisaged by John Reid-Dodick, global head of human resources for business divisions, to support the programme was designed to tap into, engage and re-motivate social, innovation, expert, career guidance and learning networks that were made up of well-educated, sophisticated but highly cynical media professionals.

Fast Forward: the context

In 2001 Reuters was in the middle of a conventional top-down change management programme designed by Tom Glocer, the new chief executive, to alter the company from one structured around geographical markets to one centred on a global series of products. Unfortunately, it was derailed by a sudden and unanticipated collapse in Reuters' markets brought about in part by the dotcom crisis and a consequent reappraisal of the number and type of database services used by Reuters' clients.

Before the crisis there was enough elasticity in the market for clients to use competing service providers side-by-side, Reid-Dodick explains. The crisis forced clients to make "zero-sum-game" choices:

> The main impact it had was on our competitive relationship
> with our main rival, Bloomberg. Clients were forced to choose
> between us – and while we retained some contracts, far more
> than we would have liked went to Bloomberg.

The resulting fallout led to one of the grimmest periods of retrenchment in the company's 154-year history. By February 2003, it had reported a net loss of £394m for the year ending in December 2002 – its biggest ever – and announced the cutting of 3,000 jobs. In the following three years – the period during which the Fast Forward programme was conceived, designed and launched – a further 3,000 jobs were lost.

Glocer's response was to commission an upgraded and expanded version of the organisational change programme which aimed to:

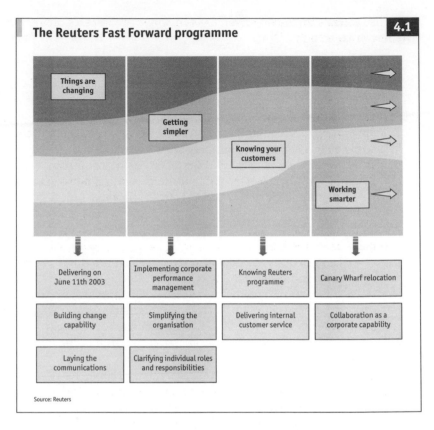

The Reuters Fast Forward programme 4.1

Things are changing

Getting simpler

Knowing your customers

Working smarter

Delivering on June 11th 2003	Implementing corporate performance management	Knowing Reuters programme	Canary Wharf relocation
Building change capability	Simplifying the organisation	Delivering internal customer service	Collaboration as a corporate capability
Laying the communications	Clarifying individual roles and responsibilities		

Source: Reuters

- make Reuters' information indispensable;
- move the business to a single-product distribution business structure;
- simplify the product line and reshape the cost base;
- focus business solutions on the products;
- invigorate the culture and behaviour of Reuters' people.

The transformation programme that resulted, called Fast Forward, is shown in Figure 4.1. It is designed to support the restructure of the company into four global customer segments and integrate the organisation's development, infrastructure, content, sales, marketing and other activities into aligned global "centres of excellence" or business services. One important focus is the creation of a new culture, based on being fast, accountable, service-driven and team-focused, or FAST.

The rationale for the programme was outlined by Glocer in an internal report in early 2004:[7]

> *Many organisational change programmes fail because they address only structural issues and do not focus enough attention on engaging their people in the process. Reuters recognised this in itself. One of the six workstreams of the transformation programme was focused on reinvigorating Reuters' culture and introducing a new way of working. This workstream was given a name and brand of its own: Living FAST – FAST stands for Fast, Accountable, Service-Driven and Team – encapsulating the values that would drive a Living FAST way of working.*
>
> *Reuters was in survival mode. To fight back, we had to take a cynical workforce with low morale and turn it into a force that was driven, looking to the future rather than the past. We needed to break down functional silos, engender a strong service ethic and focus people on building a successful company that would protect the jobs of 13,000, rather than focusing on job losses. The three-year clock had started ticking. We needed to do something quickly that would get across the sense of urgency, get everyone on the same page and involve ALL employees in driving change.*

The crucial difference in the Fast Forward programme was the change in behaviour it was intended to inculcate in the workforce. The main emphasis of the organisational change programme had been structural. Although this priority was rolled into the Fast Forward programme, the new thrust was to engender the ability to anticipate and respond to continuous change, not just among the senior management team but throughout the whole workforce.

Fast Forward: design and execution priorities
The Fast Forward programme has been central to the company's revival. It was predicated on four design strengths.

Design strength 1: a comprehensive staff consultation strategy
The priorities in each stage of the programme were determined by an online consultation exercise that identified 1,700 issues based on staff perceptions of the company's products, business practices, management style and structure. This was distilled into an agenda for a "Living FAST"

day held on June 11th 2003, in which staff quizzed senior managers on the same issues face to face.

The feedback from these exercises was submitted to a cross-functional group of 30 managers responsible for drawing up a set of design priorities for the Fast Forward development team. A two-day meeting of the group, held in July 2003, was attended by Glocer and the specifications for the programme were refined using a combination of (at the time) lively plenary discussions with Glocer and syndicate work groups on practical design and implementation issues.

No consultation exercise of this kind – aimed at a cynical workforce with low morale – had been attempted on such a scale and at such a pace. Speedy execution was essential, as Reid-Dodick explains:

> The team's task was to bring it to reality, building a realistic plan that could be delivered within six weeks in all offices and outline the budget requirements also. It had to be delivered before the end of June for two reasons: we wanted to start and maintain momentum quickly, and secondly, from the middle of June the company would enter the closed period on the run into its interim results in July and we wanted to be as open as possible in our communications on the day. We also asked the team to challenge us if they did not feel this was the right approach. In two days after working through a range of issues, scenarios and ideas, they produced the proposal, plan and budget. We were confident that we had an excellent plan produced by employees for our employees, but it was very ambitious. The central idea was to mobilise the Reuters world in one day, June 11th, where activities would begin when the sun came up in the East and end on the West Coast of America – following the sun.

The objectives were to:

- build understanding of the overall transformation programme and win commitment;
- kick-start Living FAST by building understanding of the FAST values and explaining what Living FAST means for the company and individuals and why it is central to achieving the transformation aims;
- involve employees in driving change, identifying barriers to progress, as well as generating potential solutions.

The project had a central team that provided strategic direction, communications advice and materials, managed the budget and was accountable for the delivery of the plan. It was supported by regional and local implementation teams that consisted of an army of volunteers who were excited about the concept and committed to delivering it, even though this would mean a lot of extra work.

The regional leaders were part of the central core team and were a crucial communications link with the local implementation teams. A special website was also created for the project team providing a one-stop shop for materials, messages, toolkits and support. The plan that was devised for June 11th set out to achieve a good balance between interactivity and show-and-tell and involved:

1 A welcome session presented by a senior local host lasting around 40 minutes. This was to give an overview of the transformation programme and would contain videos of the workstream leaders and the chief executive.
2 Two cross-functional interactive sessions – one on what Living FAST really meant, in which employees could say what they felt needed to be done to live FAST, and one to address specific issues or challenges set by the chief executive. Each session would last an hour, though there was flexibility about the amount of time that people could spend on the second session.
3 A 20-hour Reuters television broadcast on June 11th, streamed to employees' desktops. Essentially this was the glue that joined the Reuters world together. It would be supported by a website to carry stories and photos of activities around the world.

Employees were expected to spend around four hours participating in the three core elements, but they were free to spend longer if they wished. The designers also encouraged the organising teams to arrange extra fun activities.

To help shape the content for June 11th and to get a real feel for the barriers to progress, Reuters ran a worldwide issues audit in May. An online database on the Living FAST website gave everyone in the company the opportunity to register their issues – with the caveat that they had to suggest a solution. The audit ran for two weeks and drew more than 3,000 individual responses.

Employees were asked to register comments in nine topic areas ranging from products and organisational issues to marketing and customer service. To demonstrate commitment to credible, meaningful, two-way dialogue, the company set itself a target of five days to collate the results, report back and then allocate every issue to a senior manager who became responsible for following it up. The key themes or issues raised helped form the content for June 11th and the challenges that would be addressed via the interactive cross-functional workshops. Reid-Dodick explains:

> We knew we needed to create events that gave every participant
> the chance to feel connected to our global strategy and ambitions.
> Equally, we knew those activities had to feel locally owned and
> driven. Our response was to develop workshops that would
> be carefully structured and simple to allow local facilitators
> to work with their teams to address local and global issues.
> Workshop formats were created and tested as local facilitators
> were identified. Each facilitator was given a detailed briefing and
> training materials ready for the day itself.

Design strength 2: dedicated (and branded) communications tools
To support the consultation exercise and bring the strategy to life, Reuters used all the media expertise and technology at its disposal. What it produced and disseminated included branded posters, screensavers, backdrops, stationery and regular newsletters that could be downloaded from the project team's website.

A Living FAST website was created to provide a reference point for all Living FAST global and local activities and to develop a sense of anticipation through interactive features and news updates from the organising teams. The site would also become the homepage for everyone in the organisation on June 11th. Employees around the world were encouraged to send reports and pictures of their activities to a pool of website editors.

The project team set up a studio in London for the TV broadcast and carried out extensive testing to make sure that employees could receive the stream and that it would work on the day. State-of-the-art streaming technology enabled Reuters' staff to tune in on their desktops, while smaller offices without a full IT infrastructure could watch via a secure website encoded by BT. A television programme schedule and pre-recorded material were also produced.

After six weeks of intense preparation, on June 11th 2003 most employees arrived to find their offices transformed by locally and globally produced Living FAST campaign materials. A breakfast meeting began with a welcome from the local host, who set the tone and outlined the expectations for the day. This included a personal video message from the chief executive, Tom Glocer, and an overview of the transformation programme, which led into the first workshop about Living FAST. With the global broadcast under way, everyone could return to their desks and follow events as they unfolded to whatever degree they were able. Local activities throughout the day gave people the opportunity to work together in other ways related to Living FAST.

In the afternoon everyone gathered for another workshop, based on a set of challenges to the organisation from Glocer called "Tom's Challenges", drawn from the issues auditing process. Workshop teams could choose one challenge for discussion and feedback. The overall approach was flexible enough to allow small offices to participate fully in the day; for example, some smaller offices joined in the workshops by teleconference.

To justify the time and effort every employee gave to the workshops, there had to be a way to share their conclusions in a manner that drove development and results. Workshop leaders put the feedback, suggestions and ideas into a special database for all to see. On the day, 1,300 cross-functional groups addressed the issues and made proposals.

Three presenters fronted the 20-hour television marathon, supported by a team of producers, directors and technicians, to create a broadcast that was technically excellent and which generated an enthusiastic response.

Design strength 3: dedicated organisational learning and individual development
Feedback from the Living FAST day made it clear to senior managers that many employees felt they did not know enough about the company, its customers and its structure. To help solve this problem, the company built a sophisticated learning service. This was designed and launched by a newly appointed global head of learning, Charles Jennings, one of a group of specialists brought in to advise the company during the early stages of the consultation process.

On the back of the Living FAST day, Jennings launched Knowing Reuters, an eight-hour online learning programme that every employee is expected to complete. This is followed up with a diagnostic test and an accreditation process. In conjunction with Knowing Reuters, he introduced a version of Books 24X7, a support reference tool for Reuters' 2,000 technical staff. After a successful trial, it was rolled out to 1,600 people. Its website provides the full text of 3,000 reference books, backed up by a search engine. Jennings also revamped the old internal management directory, which feedback had indicated was one of the few tools that employees relied on to break out of their departmental silos.

Reuters also rethought the middle manager competencies required to support the Fast Forward strategy. A new in-company management programme, Leading Edge, focused on leadership, personal accountability and decision-making in the context of the four FAST values of being fast, accountable, service driven and team-oriented.

Each day of Leading Edge focused on one of these values. Delegates were organised into working groups to examine real business issues related to that value. The programme culminated in a wrap-up session on the final day (called "So What Are You Going to Do?") in which delegates made a commitment to a personal course of action related directly to one or more of the Fast Forward goals. One important feature was presentations by senior managers, who were told to base their contributions on personal experience and to provide an honest view of the business and its prospects.

Design strength 4: calculated social network analysis
From the moment Fast Forward was envisaged, Glocer and Reid-Dodick recognised that one of Reuters' organisational strengths was how highly networked it was and how tapping these networks could be a driving force in executing Glocer's change strategy.

Although Stephenson's concept of social network analysis was not known to either at the time, its operational philosophy – that senior managers of change should be appointed on the basis of their networking ability and not just their position in the formal hierarchy – was uppermost in their minds.

The manager chosen to chair the steering committee overseeing Fast Forward was Graham Albutt, head of the business technology group. This was a cross-functional unit supporting all the main business departments and thus, in Stephenson's lexicon, a key "hub" of the organisation. This allowed Albutt to act as both a "pulse-taker" of employee attitudes and a "gatekeeper" for all important messages from the senior management team. Reid-Dodick says:

> *Tom showed extraordinary insight in picking Graham for the job. Graham knew the business and the technology but he had also built an incomparable network of relationships as a result of working in both Britain and America and extensive travel in Asia over a 15-year period.*

In turn, Albutt selected 30–40 highly networked junior and middle managers to act as the main gatekeepers of the messages initially developed at the March 2003 management conference. They were deliberately redistributed throughout the organisation and their feedback that the frontline staff wanted to be more actively involved in the execution of the strategy prompted the steering committee to propose the consultation day that took place on June 11th. The effectiveness of these gatekeepers in using their networks to gain support for the Living FAST day also enabled the company to plan, design and run the event in just six weeks.

Glocer's ability to take the pulse of the senior managers attending the March 17th conference was also demonstrated by an appeal to delegates to support the Fast Forward initiative by pledging to buy Reuters shares using yellow Post-It notes. (Reuters share price was at a record low at the time.) Glocer would not have risked such a high-profile appeal had he and other members of the steering group not picked up that there was a groundswell of confidence in how he was planning to improve the company's fortunes. Had the appeal fallen on stony ground, it could have brought the impetus driving the initiative to a shuddering halt. In the event, pledges for 500,000 shares were made on the spot, with some managers subsequently spending five-figure sums to demonstrate their support for the company.

5 Behaviour

Many companies – often unwittingly – create an environment where competition and self-interest negate skilful co-operation. But the good news is that much of this can be changed. We can craft the practices and processes of our companies to favour co-operation rather than competition – and keep our best talent effectively engaged in the process.

Lynda Gratton, professor of management practice, London Business School

Luncheon Vouchers in 1989: creating a competitive environment

When Luncheon Vouchers was acquired in 1989 by Accor, a French hotels and catering giant, the new managing director, Olivier de Bosredon, discovered quickly that the staff were demotivated and lacked initiative.

The reason was simple: Luncheon Vouchers was the only company in the UK selling tax-free vouchers that employers could redeem for food at restaurants and sandwich bars. But it was a monopoly supplier because British tax regulations governing the distribution of meal tickets to staff by their employers did not give a sufficient profit margin to providers. This left Luncheon Vouchers alone in the market, in marked contrast to overseas meal-ticket companies which were locked in a lively and increasingly international market. With no other company to provide a direct threat or point of comparison, there was little incentive for staff either to maintain a high level of productivity or to be inventive.

Working with Sue Harvey, the company's sales and marketing director, de Bosredon came up with a novel solution. The company organised a two-week competition during which all staff were invited to compare their performance against counterparts in a fictitious competing organisation.

A detailed prospectus of the fictitious company was drawn up with a description of how each department was made up, details of the quality standards to which it operated and its most recent performance figures. These were pitched at levels Harvey and de Bosredon calculated that the corresponding department at Luncheon Vouchers could reach during a two-week period.

The various departments were then challenged to match or exceed these targets. Departmental and individual prizes were offered and a collective goal for all staff was set to put the competitor out of business. An internal newsletter was set up to provide daily bulletins on the battle between the companies, culminating in a full-page, front-cover article announcing the demise of the competitor when, much to the delight of de Bosredon and Harvey, the targets were all reached or exceeded.

The exercise was deemed a great success. Harvey subsequently took over the company as de Bosredon's successor. Among the many ideas put forward as a means of beating the fictitious competitor, one – suggested by one of the marketing managers – stuck in her mind. This was that Luncheon Vouchers should expand by extending the idea of meal tickets to other commodities or services. She made this the basis for her strategy in the 1990s and Accor Services UK, as the company is known, now provides a range of vouchers covering services such as childcare, eye care and dental care.

Behaviour and how it is shaped

Luncheon Vouchers was in the rare position of having no competitors in an open market, but following the takeover by Accor, De Bosredon was faced with what is a common problem: demotivated staff who lacked initiative.

The big difference between strategy execution during the final two decades of the 20th century and the task today is that previously the focus was almost exclusively on process "re-engineering", whereas now it is on how the effective achievement of key goals is shaped and underpinned by the employees' behaviour.

An individual's behaviour is shaped by a complex mix of his or her attitudes and aspirations and how these are influenced by the collective culture and protocol of an organisation. The impact of corporate policies and external factors such as the current state of local labour markets on how employees think, see, feel and thus behave has become a new area of investigation for senior management teams working closely with personnel departments.

Deutsche Bank and employee commitment: a new area of risk

Deutsche Bank, for instance, bases its performance and retention strategies on the relationship between corporate values and the way they are perceived and shared throughout the organisation through a commitment to teamwork, trust, innovation, customer focus and high performance. Each individual's level of commitment is assessed by three measures:

- the degree of willingness to perform beyond the usually expected level (engagement);

47

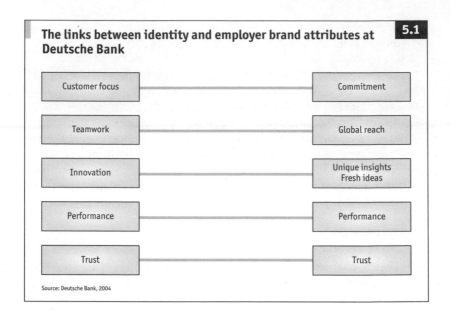

The links between identity and employer brand attributes at Deutsche Bank `5.1`

Customer focus	Commitment
Teamwork	Global reach
Innovation	Unique insights Fresh ideas
Performance	Performance
Trust	Trust

Source: Deutsche Bank, 2004

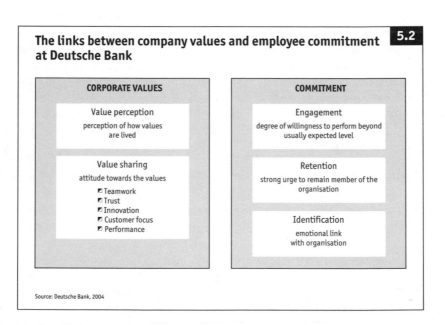

The links between company values and employee commitment at Deutsche Bank `5.2`

CORPORATE VALUES

Value perception

perception of how values are lived

Value sharing

attitude towards the values

- Teamwork
- Trust
- Innovation
- Customer focus
- Performance

COMMITMENT

Engagement

degree of willingness to perform beyond usually expected level

Retention

strong urge to remain member of the organisation

Identification

emotional link with organisation

Source: Deutsche Bank, 2004

◼ the urge to remain part of the organisation (retention);
◼ emotional involvement with the organisation (identification).

The commitment index developed by Deutsche Bank is illustrated in Figures 5.1 and 5.2.

An assessment of how "committed" employees are at any given time is undertaken through a periodic anonymous attitude survey (see Table 5.1 overleaf). This provides a pulse-take of the health of the organisation and helps identify early trends that lead to declining performance or a haemorrhaging of talent in time for line managers to identify and deal with the causes. This is crucially important to both human resources management and the bank's broader sense of operational risk, which it defines as "the potential for incurring losses through unmanageable events, business disruptions, inadequately defined controls or control/ system failure".

Although these "risks" clearly extend to the bank's dealings with its customers, suppliers, regulators and technology, staff relations are a clear priority. Potential operational risks related to employees identified by the human resources department included those influencing the motivation, adaptability, qualification and departure of individual members of the workforce. Losing the top performers within a group or division is regarded as the most serious and costly risk of all.

The commitment index has enabled the bank to link its concept of engagement and commitment with its strategic goals.[1] The ability of the survey to provide senior managers and business unit managers with reports about employees' engagement with their work, their urge to remain with the organisation and their emotional link with the bank's core values has been pivotal to its commercial success. Its contribution to the bank's ability to manage operational risk is a particularly important plank in its philosophy of "strategic readiness" (see Figure 5.3 on page 51).

Behaviour: the strategy execution challenge

In terms of strategy execution, the challenge facing senior managers in attempting to shape and influence an individual's or team's behaviour has been outlined by Julian Birkinshaw, professor of strategic and international management at London Business School.[2] He suggests that individual and team behaviour is shaped by four factors:

◼ Stretch – how individuals are stimulated to push for high-quality results and are held accountable for those results.

Table 5.1 **Issues covered by employee surveys at Deutsche Bank**

Employer of choice status	
Organisational	Co-ordination and integration
Framework	Organisational learning
Employer image	Operational efficiency
Diversity	Recognition
Leadership	Responsibility and empowerment
Strategic direction	Professional development
Co-ordination	Compensation
	Information management
Corporate identity	
Value sharing	Attitude towards the values
Value perception	Teamwork, trust and innovation
	Customer focus and performance, and attributes such as transparency and consistency
	Perception of how these values are lived
People	
Commitment	Willingness to stay
Competence	Attitude to labour market
Individual	Emotional involvement with the organisation
Adaptability	Willingness to engage
	Willingness to adapt to change
	Early warning factors

Source: Deutsche Bank, 2004

- ◪ Support – how individuals get access to the tools they need to perform.
- ◪ Space – how individuals gain the degree of freedom they need to choose their own path.
- ◪ Boundaries – the specification of clear limits beyond which the individual must not stray.

The Deutsche Bank survey framework

5.3

STRATEGIC READINESS

Processes · Markets · Financials

PEOPLE

HUMAN CAPITAL

Engagement · Retention · Identification · Competence

Individual adaptability

ORGANISATION

EMPLOYER OF CHOICE

Organisational framework
Work content
Area of responsibility
Empowerment
Operational efficiency
Team efficiency
Organisational learning
Comp. and benefits

Employer image

Diversity

Leadership
Financial and business success
Operational excellence
Franchise building
Leading people

Strategic direction and coordination
Strategic understanding
Development
Investment in skills
Coordination
Information management

Corporate identity
Value perception
Value sharing
▪ Trust
▪ Performance
▪ Innovation
▪ Teamwork
▪ Customer focus

Source: Deutsche Bank, 2004

51

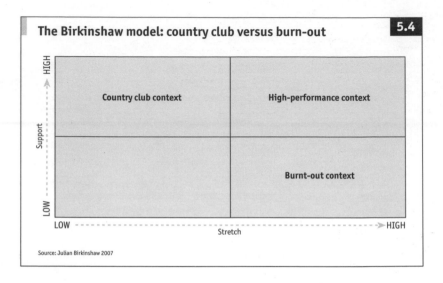

The Birkinshaw model: country club versus burn-out 5.4

Source: Julian Birkinshaw 2007

Birkinshaw argues that many companies operate either a "country-club" culture, in which support is high and stretch is low; or a "burn-out" culture, in which stretch is high but support is low. They can also veer between "bureaucratic contexts", in which boundaries are high but space is low; and "chaos", in which the reverse is true. Getting the right balance between stretching goals and the right support, and between a bureaucratic

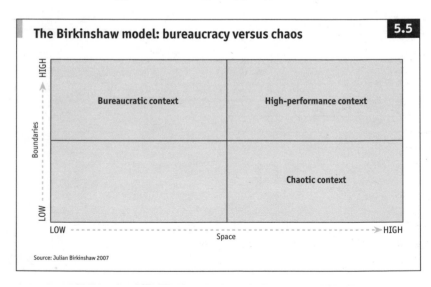

The Birkinshaw model: bureaucracy versus chaos 5.5

Source: Julian Birkinshaw 2007

and chaotic working atmosphere, is crucial to turning strategy into great performance (see Figures 5.4 and 5.5).

He points, as an illustration, to the revival of Renault by Louis Schweitzer, its chief executive, following its merger ("alliance") with Japanese carmaker Nissan in 1998:[3]

> Until 1990, employees at Renault had viewed the company
> as a comfortable and secure place to work with an informal
> atmosphere – very much like a country club. Over the following
> ten years, the company was transformed by a great focus on,
> and commitment to, key strategic objectives. Strategic goals were
> updated every two to three years, yet the organisation was also
> able to adopt an informal style of management where expressing
> alternative views was encouraged and managers developed
> a self-critical approach whereby they were always looking to
> improve.

Mirroring the experiences of Luxfer Gas Cylinders (see Chapter 3), a greater focus on new products and opportunities at Renault, Birkinshaw argues, in turn generated a freer operational style. Indeed, two of the goals championed by Schweitzer – "Develop a coherent and open group" and "Work more effectively together" – were aimed at producing this result.

Coaching and personal support: the learning agenda

The experiences of Renault and LGC provide a template for the coaching and support systems companies need to set in place to make sure strategic goals and missions are executed successfully. This encompasses:

- a unifying focus on the main goals/mission of the strategy;
- a focus on customers and competition;
- an emphasis on effective teamwork and individual initiative;
- clarity in how individuals see their own role in achieving the main goals/mission of the strategy – and in the role of their colleagues and collaborators;
- a culture of collaboration among individuals, teams, work units, suppliers and other stakeholders.

The balance between focused goals and freedom to operate is critical. Birkinshaw concludes:[4]

Success is dependent on "driving leadership" rather than being "leadership-driven". It arises not just through formal structure, nor through the vision statements of a charismatic leader. Rather, it is achieved in large part through the creation of a supportive context in which individuals make their own choices about how and where to focus their energies.

The Asian strategy of a global branded drinks company

A good example is how one global branded drinks company (which requested anonymity to protect commercial confidentiality) achieved these goals in the context of a highly competitive regional market in which competition between different brands and the companies that produce them is cut-throat.

The company faced a much stronger, more focused competitor which, at the time of the initiative, was the market leader. It knew, or had access to, a significant amount of information about the competition, but traditionally its strategy had been focused on its own consumers and customers.

Senior managers had limited capability to collect and collate data and understand the competitive environment. As a result, real insight existed only in discrete pockets around the region lower down in the organisation. This made it difficult for the company's region-wide management to co-ordinate a competitor-focused strategy. The lack of knowledge, as opposed to data, also made it challenging to create a more competitive edge, together with greater confidence and awareness of how the competition could be beaten.

To generate better awareness of its rivals throughout the organisation, senior managers designed a training and coaching initiative, which they called the counter competitive programme, based on the way military commanders sift and analyse the intelligence available to them.

The counter competitive programme

This was implemented over 12 months from February 2005. The first element was a fundamental review or estimate of the competitive environment and the threats facing the company. The insights of this review were integrated into the company's medium-term strategy and the main goals or missions of the strategy were then subjected to a "battle rehearsal" held in June 2005.

The regional and market leadership teams and their strategies were tested against "live" adversaries in the form of an expert team simulating the likely activities of the competition and events taking place in the marketplace. "Players" in the exercise were forced to cope with the demands of unpredictable economic and external affairs events as well as trying successfully to execute their declared strategy.

Objectives
The objectives of the programme were to:

- build confidence that the team could achieve their objectives during 2006;
- build the quality of their responses and reactions;
- develop behaviours that were adaptable and flexible;
- support the regional strategy;
- develop the sense of everyone being part of a regional team.

Results
The counter competitor programme was designed to produce a more effective strategic planning process in which overall goals could be translated into short – and medium-term objectives that, in turn, could be distilled into individual and team tasks capable of being measured and tracked. It also provided managers at various levels with the leadership skills they needed to keep their staff, as one participant put it, "onside and on track".

Its main benefit, however, was to highlight the lack of awareness among all staff of their competitors' strategic intentions and ways of working. As one marketing manager commented:

It was a brilliant tool to help us understand the strengths and vulnerabilities of our own strategy and to highlight what needed to be changed and adjusted.

As a result of the exercise, the company's plans were adjusted and the teams' understanding of the revised strategy retested using the same exercise. The consultancy that designed the exercise was also rehired to develop a new framework for analysing competitor intelligence and to support decision-making at every level of the organisation.

Internal and external consultancy support: the changing agenda

The counter competitive programme illustrates how the role of consultants is changing.

In the 1980s and 1990s consultants saw themselves as "thought leaders", competing with academic business gurus to shape the thinking and mindset of the senior managers who created their strategies. But the work undertaken by their counterparts today is often more "down and dirty", working with managers two or three layers down to make sure that the main goals and missions of the strategy are properly appreciated and that people understand their own roles, and the roles of their colleagues and collaborators, in achieving these goals. Damian McKinney of McKinney Rogers stresses:

> *Strategies can only be sustained by clarity of purpose, and clarity can only be achieved through changes in behaviour. The capacity for people two or three layers down to get the wrong end of the stick is never ending and constantly reinforced by poor management. Persistent but sensitive vigilance is needed to check false perceptions and over-interpretation of simple objectives.*
>
> *To this end, coaching and feedback are integral to our partnership with clients. We spend 80% of our time on this activity. We try to provide a "lifeline" to key teams and projects, enabling individuals to reach out for one-to-one support to maintain momentum and progress when working with business realities.*

He is not alone is stressing this role. Sean Connolly, a senior consultant at Egremont Consulting, which specialises in change management, comments:[5]

> *In the old days, consultancies pitched for large-scale, process-based contacts. My perception is that what clients are now looking for is more focused – consultants working in smaller teams on a myriad of small-scale engagements that demonstrate to people throughout the organisation how their behaviour and actions contribute to the overall picture.*

Sue Grist, also a consultant at Egremont Consulting, adds:[6]

> *You have to work directly with each team leader, demonstrating how they promote and support the strategy. Teams often need a lot of support – so that when they start to nurse an idea about how they can deliver against their objectives, somebody can sit down with them and help them explore it. What you now roll out is not the solution, what you roll out is the discovery process.*

From coaching to measurement

One of the most important roles of modern consultancies is helping their clients set up the internal systems they need to be able to measure how successful their efforts at strategy execution are and to co-ordinate and focus support where it is most needed.

Palladium, a consultancy set up by performance measurement and alignment experts Robert Kaplan and David Norton, has helped a number of organisations set up strategy co-ordination centres called the office of the chief executive, modelled on military general staff headquarters. These include two organisations discussed in this book: Luxfer Gas Cylinders (see Chapter 3) and HSBC Rail (see Chapter 6).

Most commercial organisations do not have a process or an individual responsible for managing strategy, notes Norton. It is usually a responsibility scattered across functions, rather as (in information technology) the role of the chief information officer was undertaken in the 1980s.

The idea of a central co-ordinating "strategy office" was championed by Chrysler in the early 1990s. A designated manager was given responsibility for liaising with different businesses in the group to make sure that a focus on the strategic priorities was maintained. The most important roles of the strategy office are to:

- chart an overview of how various business functions contribute to the cross-disciplinary goals of the strategy, often in the form of a "strategy map";
- make sure that the performance of business units, specialist functions and external suppliers and providers is aligned with these goals;
- break down these goals into team-based and individual objectives throughout the organisation, making sure that the central focus is not lost or diluted and that everything remains aligned;
- develop the appropriate measures and milestones that will make sure that performance is appraised against these goals;
- liaise continuously with all levels of the organisation to make sure that essential resources (money, technology and people) are allocated to the projects and objectives that really contribute to these goals and are not frittered away on the pet schemes of local managers or poorly focused initiatives.

The next chapter looks at how this achieved.

6 Measurement

Identifying the key drivers of performance and forecasting the impact of the right business interventions require powerful measurement techniques. However, analysing this data is of little use if insufficient time is spent on interpreting and communicating the results internally and externally to meet different stakeholders' needs.

Jim Matthewman, worldwide partner, Mercer Human Resource Consulting

HSBC Rail (UK): charting the future through corporate cartography

Peter Aldridge, the chief executive of HSBC Rail (UK), found his company needed more strategic focus for a very simple reason: there were too many initiatives and not enough resources to go round.

HSBC Rail is a subsidiary of the HSBC banking group. It was established in the late 1990s to meet the investment and financing requirements of the passenger and freight rail industry. As well as offering a range of financing options, it provides procurement, refurbishment, engineering support and maintenance improvements for a fleet of more than 4,000 railway vehicles.

The attempt by the company's senior managers to conduct a major strategic review in 2005 proved much harder than expected. Aldridge explains:

> We found it harder than we thought it would be. Our strategy in 2005 involved the kind of activities that you might expect – reducing costs and becoming more efficient in the way we used not only our assets but also our share capital. But the way the various contributions of each function contributed to these goals was not codified effectively and didn't join up.

Part of the problem was that the limited resources available to the business – in terms of money, equipment and people – were being dispersed among more than 60 initiatives not linked to the company's strategic goals. The first outcome of the review, therefore, was the whittling back of projects to less than one-third of the original number.

Strategic Measurement Tool 1: the strategy map

To undertake the task the team, under Aldridge's personal direction, developed a strategy map to align all activities undertaken by the company's business units to a smaller cross-functional set of corporate goals, which are complex and multifaceted.

The company, which is based in London, has about 100 employees. It owns about 33% of the rolling stock of the UK's railway network. In 2005, as part of a wider refocusing on a higher return on equity within the HSBC group, HSBC Rail was required to review its business in order to restructure its balance sheet and sell assets.

To achieve this Aldridge and his team needed to identify measures to track the business's strategic performance. It quickly became apparent that to measure HSBC Rail's strategy it first had to be described – hence the need for the strategy map.

The HSBC Rail strategy map: objectives

It took six months of regular review and refinement for the senior management team to produce the strategy map. Aldridge says:

> You have to make sure you are delivering the right things to your customers in order for you, in turn, to deliver the right things for your shareholders. In turn, this forces you to ask yourself whether you are recruiting and developing the right people. The finished map looks like it took five minutes to put together and what it charts about the company looks, in retrospect, blindingly obvious and covers key tasks that you would have thought we should have known about for years. But it was very difficult to do well and get right.

The map is based on a template developed by Robert Kaplan and David Norton, the inventors of the balanced scorecard (see page 66). It channels and assesses the focus and alignment of each function's contribution to the business using four themes:

- Capital efficiency
- Customer relationship
- Operational excellence
- Learning and growth

Each theme is colour coded and all the activities and tasks under each

Defining strategic readiness: the Kaplan/Norton strategy map

6.1

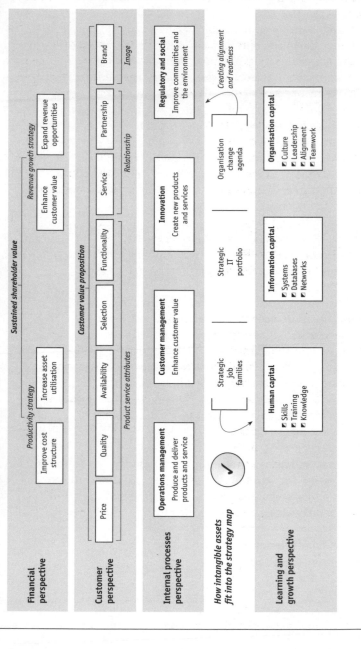

Financial perspective

Sustained shareholder value

Productivity strategy

Improve cost structure

Increase asset utilisation

Revenue growth strategy

Enhance customer value

Expand revenue opportunities

Customer perspective

Customer value proposition

Price | Quality | Availability | Selection | Functionality | Service | Partnership | Brand

Product service attributes

Relationship

Image

Internal processes perspective

Operations management
Produce and deliver products and service

Customer management
Enhance customer value

Innovation
Create new products and services

Regulatory and social
Improve communities and the environment

How intangible assets fit into the strategy map

Strategic job families

Strategic IT portfolio

Organisation change agenda

Creating alignment and readiness

Learning and growth perspective

Human capital
☑ Skills
☑ Training
☑ Knowledge

Information capital
☑ Systems
☑ Databases
☑ Networks

Organisation capital
☑ Culture
☑ Leadership
☑ Alignment
☑ Teamwork

Source: Robert Kaplan and David Norton, 2004

theme relate to the following strategic "destination", to be achieved by 2010:

> *A transition from capital intensive asset investment to delivery of a broader range of products and services which together make much more efficient use of our expertise and capital and results in improved returns on equity.*

The HSBC Rail strategy map: the measures

The activities under each theme are also linked by a series of subsidiary but equally important cross-disciplinary objectives. One crucial objective, for example, is to "develop a responsive organisation that is responsive on its feet". This entails measures of progress under each theme (see box).

HSBC Rail (UK)'s progress measures

Goal: to develop an organisation that is responsive on its feet

Key activities
- **Theme: capital efficiency** (coloured pink)
  - Develop alternative capital and funding structures
- **Theme: customer relationship management** (coloured blue)
  - Work proactively with [rail service] operators to build strong relationships and develop value-added solutions
  - Build a strong relationship with the Department of Transport and other government bodies and third-party investors
  - Build market intelligence that positions us [HSBC Rail] to be the supplier of choice for the right deals
- **Theme: operational excellence** (coloured yellow)
  - Deliver highly effective, customer-focused supplier performance
  - Continue to selectively invest resources to minimise our residual value risk
  - Focus on business process excellence to deliver improvement in productivity
- **Theme: learning and growth** (coloured green)
  - Share and implement best practices

Developing the right measures of progress under each theme was a process of trial and error. Aldridge says:

It wasn't practical for us to wait until we had the perfect measure for each objective – we never would have made a start. In some cases, we provided the overall goal and let our account managers refine it. In others, we initially set measures that looked right at the time but turned out not to be very effective.

The HSBC Rail strategy map: the reporting framework

An important principle was that the managers appointed to oversee each theme, the theme owners, had the data they needed to plot and describe progress to the management team on a regular basis. This made sure that the strategy map was the centrepiece of HSBC Rail's business reporting framework. Aldridge says:

One of the most important changes we introduced was that members of the team do not spend the whole of the meeting reporting on financial issues such as the current return on equity. Rather, each theme owner highlights the objective on the map that they are currently focusing on and how the company is performing against them.

Usually the discussion and debate is around the resources we are throwing at the objective. Have we got the right people at the right time at the right place? Does the theme owner need extra help? Have you been surprised by something and do we need to change it?

We always establish accountabilities and timeframes: Who is going to perform this or that task and when is it going to be undertaken by? This kind of review may be different from the strictly financial review we undertook in the past – but it is not undertaken any less rigorously.

Results

Although HSBC Rail has used its strategy map since 2004, it has already helped the organisation to move a long way towards meeting its 2010 goal of making more efficient use of its expertise and capital. While developing the map, the management team came up with a new approach to how the company would operate by deciding to leverage the parent bank's investment management expertise, bringing in third-party investors to finance deals for which HSBC Rail would have previously provided the capital.

This big strategic change was fully endorsed by the parent bank. It has led to a restructuring of HSBC Rail's activities and the creation of a new team within the bank's investment unit to manage future financing of rail deals. A further benefit of the programme has been the alignment of HSBC Rail's executive team around its new strategy. Particularly impressive has been the way this team has rallied around the strategy, actively involving not only HSBC Rail's employees but also those of suppliers and contractors in defining and driving the strategy through the balanced scorecard reporting system.

Strategy execution: the importance of effective performance measures

The care that Aldridge's management team took to develop the right measures of progress lies at the heart of their success in strategy execution – as it does for any organisation.

Chapter 3 described how John Rhodes of Luxfer Gas Cylinders brought together 20 managers from around the world for a week to create a roadmap that became the bible for the company's growth. It is used as the template against which any new initiative is assessed and all existing activities are regularly measured.

Yet the survey on strategy execution undertaken in 2003 by The Economist Intelligence Unit and Marakon Associates (see Chapter 2) found that faulty measurement and reporting were the main reasons why companies on average (according to the survey) achieve only 63% of the financial performance their strategies promise.

A number of defects and breakdowns in measurement and performance management are cited as particularly undermining of strategy:

- **Companies rarely track performance against long-term plans.** The survey suggests that less than 15% of companies regularly compare their results with the performance forecast for each business unit in the previous year's strategic results. As a result, managers cannot easily know whether the projections that underlie their capital-investment and portfolio-strategy decisions predict actual performance.
- **Multiyear results rarely meet projections.** When companies do track performance, it rarely matches the previous year's projection. The consequence is year after year of underperformance relative to the original plan.
- **Value is lost in translation.** A combination of poor communications, misapplied resources, limited accountability and lack of information creates a gap between strategy and

performance. Performance bottlenecks are frequently invisible to senior managers.

☑ **Strategy-to-performance gaps foster a culture of underperformance.** Unrealistic plans create the expectation throughout the organisation that plans simply will not be fulfilled. As this expectation is turned into experience, it becomes the norm that performance commitments are not kept.

Effective performance measures are all the more important because the effective execution of any strategy often requires the performance of suppliers, distributors and business partners to be aligned with the main goals of the organisation as closely as that of internal departments.

HSBC Rail (UK)'s supplier management

The importance of effective supplier management is a critical objective for HSBC Rail. "Delivering highly effective, customer-focused supplier performance" is a central target in achieving its goal of effective operational excellence. CEO Peter Aldridge describes how it is achieved.

The practical application of how we engage with our supplier community has its basis in both the vision and values of our business (having long-term ethical relationships) and our company strategy articulated through the balanced scorecard (Internal Process No. 6: deliver highly effective, customer-focused supplier relationships). While the individual statements provide focus, they also relate back into all other aspects of our business through the themes of capital efficiency, customer relationship management, operational excellence and learning and growth, which ensures that procurement is supported by and supports other business functions.

The focus provided by the balanced scorecard within our company has further infused strategy with comments, wants, needs and expectations both internally within the business and externally with our supplier and customers. This has led to rail asset and rail maintenance procurement being defined as having three functions.

1 Sourcing. "To obtain competitive advantage, best value, performance and quality for the products and services supplied to us and to our customers." This is complemented by five clear reasons of why we purchase. They are to:

☑ tangibly meet customer requirements;

- meet mandatory requirements;
- measurably improve safety;
- increase profitability;
- decrease the cost base.

This enables our people to procure in line with defined tangible business requirements that can demonstrate "a return on our investment" and that nothing we do operates in a vacuum away from those business requirements.

2 Commercial support. "We are committed to procuring responsibly in ways that build on the values and requirements of the business." Success has been identified as:

- ensuring that a specialist team effectively supports the business in our dealings with suppliers;
- being informed and able to make clear business judgments in the railway supply market;
- having the necessary skills and knowledge to evaluate and respond to conflicting demands;
- having a clear picture of our entire scope for railway goods and services.

3 Supplier management. "Develop the market to meet our needs and our customers' current and future needs." Success is to:

- deliver and maintain high-quality, cost-effective and delivery-focused suppliers;
- develop and improve suppliers' capabilities and performance;
- understand the market, stakeholders and influences;
- ensure continuity.

We have put in place clearly defined tools that provide a framework to do business that allow and foster empowerment and innovation within clear business guidelines. A specific tool that is used for both sourcing and supplier management is a supplier evaluation model. It provides the hub and media to communicate our business strategy from the balanced scorecard themes into what we tangibly need from our suppliers. The model of evaluation is referred to as four quadrants: structure, culture, enabling processes and delivery.

Each quadrant is further defined by 15 specific measures covering items such as strategic alignments, risk management and product delivery. Each measure is supported by a scoring mechanism that has statements relating to various levels of success. The scores are reported in our balanced scorecard reporting pack and in internal and customer review meetings. This allows us to consistently articulate where there are strengths and weaknesses in our relationship, which also provides areas of focus. Furthermore, it allows our suppliers to evaluate us because we have to meet our obligations as a customer.

A practical example is a new long-term bogie management programme that is one of our largest items of long-term expenditure. By using these tools we have secured repairs for our bogies (the wheels and basic frame of a carriage or wagon) for ten years on a discount basis with a single supplier. The sourcing exercise used our seven-step process. The supplier management tools (segmentation, communication strategy, account planning, market review and supplier evaluation model) are being used to develop the relationship.

Using these tools combined with others such as safety management and project management has developed an open and responsive relationship. HSBC Rail and the contractor both understand each other's needs and there is an open relationship in which the most difficult issues can be discussed without referring to a contract or creating a culture of blame. This is a developing relationship and these aspects of the balanced scorecard are being used to focus the programme and measure success:

- continuously improve productivity;
- provide long-term asset management services;
- provide a value-for-money total cost of ownership;
- provide the assets and service portfolio to support the business;
- work proactively with operators to build strong relationships and develop value-adding solutions.

The process has been fully operational for around 12 months and we are beginning to achieve real and measurable cost savings. Quality has been generally good and there are signs that it is improving with turnaround times on plan. We are now using the same system with all our other major suppliers.

Strategic Measurement Tool 2: the balanced scorecard

Both HSBC Rail and Luxfer Gas Cylinders build balanced scorecards into their strategy mapping and reporting systems. Since it was devised in the 1990s, the balanced scorecard has become the most popular means of measuring business performance. A survey by Cranfield School of Management in the early 2000s found that 75% of the companies involved use the balanced scorecard in their performance systems and that the others in the survey use a variation of it. These include organisations such as ExxonMobil, Chrysler, British Petroleum, Rolls-Royce and the Ministry of Defence.

The balanced scorecard was conceived in 1990 when Kaplan and Norton worked with representatives from a dozen manufacturing and service industries on a research project called "Measuring Performance in the Organisation of the Future". Both had engineering backgrounds and the conclusion they reached with those participating in the programme was that as the old production economy gave way to "service-and-solutions" industries, traditional measures of performance were not reflecting intangible strengths that were giving these new industries their competitive strength. These included the ability to innovate and develop new products and the ability to meet customer needs.

Historically, measures of business performance focused almost exclusively on financial results and meeting targets. Kaplan and Norton argued that, at best, these could provide only a snapshot of past performance, not a reliable indicator of how a company might be expected to perform in the future.

Essentially the scorecard looks at a business from four perspectives to help senior managers evaluate performance using the following questions:

◩ The customer: How do our customers see us?
◩ Internal business: At which processes and competencies do we need to excel?
◩ Innovation and learning: Can we continue to improve and excel?
◩ Financial: How do we look to our shareholders?

An example based on Reuters' use of balanced scorecards (see Chapters 4 and 8) is provided in Figure 6.2 overleaf.

Designing a scorecard should take about four months, although lack of consensus about some aspects (for example, what customers think) might result in it taking slightly longer, as happened at HSBC Rail (see above).

The perspectives used in the balanced scorecard are important for two reasons:

◩ They can be linked back to the vision, mission or objectives that provide the focus for a modern strategy. In the case of Luxfer Gas Cylinders this was the shift in its profit base from commoditised products to new, customer-focused ones. In the case of HSBC Rail, it was delivering a broader range of products and services to make

A balanced scorecard used at Reuters — 6.2

	Summary of objective	Measure	Group	Segment	Changed	O & T	Content	Corporate
PEOPLE	Employee engagement	Employee engagement index	●	■	■	■	■	■
	Employee capability	Voluntary high performers turnover	●	■	■	■	■	■
	Organisational alignment	Gap between organisational effectiveness milestone targets and actual	●	○	○	○	○	○
	Compliance	SOX compliance	●	■	■	■	■	■
CUSTOMER	Materially improve customer satisfaction	Customer satisfaction survey improvement	●	○	○	○	○	○
		Global great service index	●	○	●	○		
	Grow market share	Cross segment market share	●	●				
	Strengthen the brand	Brand tracking survey	●					
BUSINESS	Disaster recovery	Gap between target tiered service reliability and actual tier scores	●		●			
	Deliver the new business architecture	Manage full tick IDN network at 250k updates per second	●		●			
		Removal of a percentage of Reuters desktops by year end	●		●			
		US regional product cost reduction	●	●	●	●	●	
	Transform customer administration	Number of customers migrated to Order to Cash	●		●			
	Transform communications infrastructure	Number of distribution servers switched off	●		●			
	New product delivery	Gap between committed RRG date and actual	●	○	○	○	○	
	Transactional capabilities within Sales & Trading	Customer take up of transactional capabilities	●	●				
	Scale our growth opportunities	Enterprise information products revenue budget	●	●	●			
		Risk revenue budget	●	●				
		Number of buy-side product accesses	●	●	●			
		China revenue budget	●	●	●			
	Develop the consumer media business	Media online review budget	●	●	●			

Source: Reuters

more efficient use of its capital, in part by developing a responsive organisation that is "light on its feet".
- They can be used at all levels of an organisation so that there is alignment between what senior management and frontline employees understand is important – the topic of Kaplan and

Norton's book *Alignment*.[1] The aim, as they explain, is for balanced scorecards to be so accessible and deep-rooted in the way performance is measured and communicated that employees have a perfect picture of how their own objectives (especially those identified in their appraisals) relate to corporate ones.

This accessibility, the authors argue, is crucial to the successful use of the balanced scorecard system. In an interview Norton commented:[2]

Frontline employees must understand the financial consequences of their decisions and actions. Senior executives must understand the drivers of long-term financial success.

In this sense, balanced scorecards, as used by innovative companies, are as much about shaping behaviour and thinking as they are about reflecting the intangible, non-financial strengths of the company.

Kit (Catherine) Jackson, a senior consultant at Palladium, a consultancy set up by Kaplan and Norton to undertake the preparatory work needed for the balanced scorecard system as well as (in the case of Luxfer Gas Cylinders and HSBC Rail) the newer breed of strategy maps, stressed the point in an interview with the author:

There has been an interesting evolution in the thinking about the way you apply balanced scorecards. The traditional thinking is that you develop and apply very strong measures and have a very robust framework, all linked to targets, with a bonus if you meet them.

But we have found in the work we undertake with companies that having a robust balanced scorecard framework is not enough in itself. Executives have to change the way they manage. They have to change the way they think. They have to ask themselves: "What does the feedback we are getting from the scorecard tell us about the way the business is evolving? What does it tell us about the way our customers' needs are changing and how do we need to adapt our strategy as a result? What new things does it tell us about our strengths – for example, the ability of our business units to innovate or develop new ideas – and how should we shift resources to leverage these strengths more effectively?"

Many managers are still obsessed with measures and targets

*and how these apply across the business, rather than thinking
about the whole business and how the feedback they are getting
applies across all functions. The strength of companies such as
HSBC Rail and Luxfer Gas Cylinders is that they have taught
themselves to think in this holistic way and therefore make better
use of the data that the balanced scorecard framework yields.*

British Telecom: aligning human resources to the business strategy

An interesting illustration of how alignment works in practice is the
way BT Group's human resources team aligned the company's people
management strategy with the missions outlined in its 2003–04 strategy.
The team's strategy process and business planning model, developed in
the early 2000s, is designed to integrate five elements that help shape the
company's goals and key activities:

- strategic imperatives;
- individual line-of-business operational drivers;
- implications of transformational and operational change on BT
  people;
- the human resources department's strategic responses/
  interventions/deliverables;
- the functional and cost factors implicit in the human resources
  business model, including the outsourcing of all transactional and
  shared service activities and the continuous professionalisation of
  the human resources team.

Strategic imperatives

BT's operational strategy revolves around building partnerships with
customers. Its priorities include:

- keeping a relentless focus on improving customer satisfaction;
- achieving competitive advantage through cost leadership;
- putting broadband at the heart of BT;
- leading in network-based solutions based on its International
  Communications Technology (a BT brand);
- creating mobility services and solutions;
- reinventing its traditional business;
- transforming its network for the 21st century;
- motivating its people and living up to the company's values.

Business drivers

These vary to reflect the nature of the customer relationship, the market focus and the maturity of BT's businesses. For example, BT Retail's business priorities are dominated by the renewed focus on customer satisfaction, continued efforts to grow market share from an already stable position and a continued drive to improve "end-to-end" process management. BT's Global Services' strategy is dominated by a focus on re-entering and establishing new markets while improving the services and business solutions offered to clients operating in numerous locations.

People implications

Transformation and the challenges and opportunities it brings affect all those choosing to work in competitive markets, and BT's employees are no exception. Advances in technology, lifestyle shifts, demographic trends and globalisation mean changes in the way people live, work, communicate and behave. Change is a fact of life and the pace of change is relentless. BT requires its employees to adapt and grow constantly. This involves changes in vision, values, leadership capabilities, relationship management, skills, performance and employee engagement.

BT's people strategy sets out to create an inclusive, skilled, high-performing workforce of engaged and motivated people, who keep pace with and adapt to change, share a common sense of purpose, have a passion for customers and live up to the company's ideals.

Human resources strategy

Addressing these needs called for a major overhaul of existing policies, processes and personnel programmes. The human resources leadership team played a pivotal role in interpreting the requirements, shaping the strategy and designing the solutions that would deliver transformational change and enhanced organisational capability, generate greater returns from the company's investment in people and develop higher employee engagement.

The first year's agenda was intensive and ambitious. It involved tackling the redefinition and alignment of the BT brand promise and company values; redefining and recalibrating leadership capabilities and standards; overhauling talent management across the group; reinforcing the high-performance management ethic; and refocusing the group's reward strategies. All five priorities were grounded in BT's values of trust, helpfulness, inspiration, straightforwardness and heart.

Using the strategic alignment framework outlined in Figure 6.3 on page 73, the human resources leadership team embarked on consultations with line managers, senior managers, business partners such as Accenture and others from outside the company involved in human resources management, and set up a series of strategy workshops. From this the team put what it decided were the priorities into a sequential process of group-wide agenda-setting covering socialisation or commitment, performance standards and measurement, solution design, change tactics and results. Behind these were the plans and targets for individual divisions to determine workloads for the year ahead.

The approach was underpinned by the leadership team's commitment to a "distributed" leadership model, in which corporate and departmental human resources directors share collective ownership of the group strategic agenda, the business model and professional standards for the whole function. The leadership of programmes or initiatives is allocated to different members of the leadership team, making sure that accountability is across the board. They share ownership for the results and resource deployment and bridge the divide between headquarters and line management. Margaret Savage, director of human resources strategy and systems, says:

> Previously we operated in a traditional "centre versus line",
> "them and us" way, sub-optimising our contribution to the
> business. We now share responsibilities, and line human
> resource departments need to understand not only their own
> business drivers, but also how this fits into the overall BT picture
> and how the initiative they are leading benefits all. Together, we
> champion strategic alignment, cultural fit and personal growth.

Three other interlinked principles underpin this strategy alignment concept. It is designed to be replicable both down and across the businesses; it is iterative and interactive; and it is built for adaptation and sustainability. For example, a scheduled review of the original five interventions found that although the three designed to transform the company's values, leadership capability and talent were all going well and that the first phase in revitalising rewards was nearing completion, slow progress was being made on transforming performance.

This was important because new issues and challenges were surfacing that the human resources team needed to tackle. The review allowed the leadership team to reassign resources to help improve performance, make sure that plans in hand were completed, and agree the priorities

BT's strategic alignment framework

6.3

THE JOURNEY

Strategic context → *Change levers* → *Programmes*

BUSINESS ENVIRONMENT

PEOPLE

BT Strategic Context

A relentless focus on improving customer satisfaction

Achieve competitive advantage via cost leadership

Put broadband at the heart of BT

Lead the market in network-based ICT solutions

Create mobility services and solutions

Reinvent our traditional business

Transform our network for the 21st century

Motivate our people and live the values

BT Group HR Priorities

Cost transformation
- Peoplesoft 8 and AHRS

Leadership
- Talent and succession
- Graduates

Strategic sourcing
- Resourcing, exits and skills

Horizontal programmes
- My customer
- Values

Driving performance
- Managing poor performance
- Driving high performance

Reward and recognition
- New reward framework
- Hardwired scorecards

Training
- ALS and training portfolio
- Preferred supplier status

Employee relations
- Transformational change agenda
- CARE
- Balanced workforce
- Health and safety
- Sick absence and accidents

Group Ops HR Priorities

Horizontal programmes
- My customer
- Embed the values and capabilities

Cost transformation
- Peoplesoft 8 and AHRS
- Project SAM

Leadership
- Talent, succession and development fora
- Development centres and profiling
- Graduates and industrial placements
- Professionalism (HR and legal)

Strategic sourcing
- Resourcing, exits and surplus and TLC

Driving performance
- Raising performance

Reward and recognition
- New reward framework and regional pay
- Hardwired scorecards and workshops

Training
- Training portfolio and suppliers

Employee relations
- Transformational (ER/IR)
- CARE
- Balanced workforce
- Communications

Set the agenda → Establish performance requirements → Build change strategy → Align → Deliver

Source: Optima Publishing, 2004

for the coming year that centred on accelerating growth in new revenue areas such as International Communications Technology, broadband and mobility. The review also helped to improve efficiency and cost leadership by eradicating duplication and overlaps, as well as simplifying processes, reducing complexity and increasing flexibility and responsiveness.

Human resources business model

Strategic sourcing and skills/resources/total labour cost modelling capabilities are seen as critical to BT's success, and the company recognises that its human resources function needs to improve its own strategic, analytical, project management and transformational change skills. The human resources team have invested in their own systems to improve transparency, consistency and access to relevant information in order to improve decision-making.

They are adapting to the call for an enhanced standard operating environment and greater, automated self-service capabilities to enable line managers to manage people well and BT's employees to take greater control of their working lives. Like all BT's support functions, the human resources managers are simultaneously required to reduce operating costs and optimise services.

Strategic Measurement Tool 3: the mission dashboard

A third measurement tool used by a small but influential number of companies is the mission dashboard, a tool developed by McKinney Rogers to help people at all levels of an organisation keep track of the contribution they are making to their organisation's most important strategic objectives (see Chapter 3).

The dashboard gives all users a one-page performance overview of the business. It focuses on each individual's goals and targets, with indicators to measure progress towards them. All dashboards are accessed through a centrally located service. Users are able to view their dashboard and mission goals via Internet Explorer and Microsoft Outlook. Edits through the web interface give users the ability to input their own data whenever they want.

Mission dashboards are used by many of Diageo's drinks distributors, at the company's behest. Using the dashboard, employees at Judge & Dolph, one of Diageo's main American distributors, are able to keep a clear eye on their progress towards the missions and sub-missions agreed with their division. These in turn are linked to the overall mission set by the company.

Before 2003, Judge & Dolph had focused on being the leading distributor of wine and spirits in Illinois. By using the new Diageo contract and the openings it created, Julian Burzynski, the chief executive, moved the company's sights from maintaining its position as Illinois's leading distributor to being the leading drinks distributor in the United States.

The company's mission is to deliver a "visible" step change in performance – measured by both sales of cases and net sales value points – to become the premier distributor of wines and spirits in the United States. Linked to this goal are two others: to become a "$1 billion company" by turnover; and "to win the war on visibility" (a goal linked to the company's need to distinguish itself from its competitors).

This was broken down into individual missions for each division. For instance, the sales team of the company's Regal Division has been set the goal of delivering "$1.2m in TP in order to achieve the ambition of becoming a $1 billion company" (TP is an internal measure of sales volume). By contrast, the mission of Regal's off-premises division is to "deliver flawless execution that grows key accounts, beats the competition and wins the war on visibility in order to deliver a visible step change in business performance".

The dashboard highlights all these sub-missions in a way that is immediately apparent to everyone who uses it (see Figure 6.4 overleaf). It is reviewed weekly by the Regal Division and is used by Judge & Dolph's extended leadership team to make decisions across the company. It is also used during regular reviews with Diageo, the company's main client.

Burzynski feels this process has been crucial to the company's ability to stick to its targets:

> We needed transparency. The distribution industry is very secretive and there is often little information available on how you are doing. People face fires every day. When they turn on the dashboard, everybody knows how their performance is progressing against the plan. Using the dashboard, we were able to set clearly visible targets, first on a monthly and now on a daily basis. So the need to put out the daily fire is no longer an excuse and does not interfere with overall business performance.

Another organisation has used the mission dashboard to help customers' use of one its principal products.

The mission dashboard: a worked example

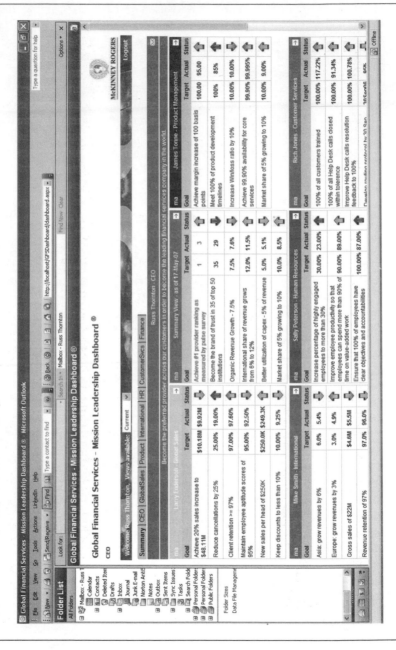

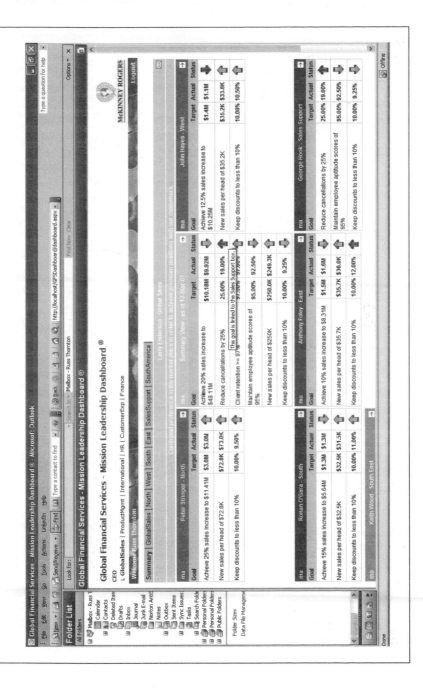

Thomson Financial: using clear measures to achieve great performance

Achieving the kind of clarity and focus that leads to better performance has been rendered very hard for companies operating across global markets because of two characteristics of recent growth and competition.

The first is a constantly shifting working population. It is far more common, for example, for knowledge-based service industries in cut-throat markets to grow through mergers and acquisitions than to grow organically. This is a prime reason for the marriage of Reuters and Thomson Financial announced in spring 2007. The process means that workforces have to be integrated into an already diverse mix of employees, up to half of which may be outsourced workers, contractors and agency staff.

The second is the cultural and turf-based barriers present in many of the organisations profiled in this book. These arise as companies move away from the functional and geographical structures that survived rapid business growth in the 1980s and the headlong rush into new markets in Asia and eastern Europe in the 1990s, and towards seamless transnational structures based on the delivery of globally available products or services.

Sarah Dunn confronted this challenge when she became European vice-president, human resources, at Thomson Financial in May 2005. The company, which provides financial information and data analysis to clients around the world, had been on a spending spree in the preceding years. Dunn says:

> We probably had made 70–80 acquisitions over the years, a situation that created disparate cultures within the organisation. Because of this, goals were not always clear and there was poor alignment with overall strategy in many of our most important work units.

However, a disparate work culture was not the only company challenge she needed to confront. One of the byproducts of the bursting of the high-tech bubble in 2001 was a reappraisal of the number and type of database services commonly used by Thomson Financial's clients. There had been enough elasticity in the market for clients to use competing services side-by-side, but the crisis forced them to make zero-sum-game choices. As a result, Thomson Financial found itself in head-to-head competition with Reuters (see Chapter 8) and Bloomberg. The bitter rivals each rationalised their services dramatically. Product differentiation had become a critical competitive strength.

Thomson Financial's response to increasing competition was a new technological tool, Thomson ONE, which enables clients to tailor and access more effectively the vast array of financial data, analytical information, research, calculations and news available on its database. What distinguishes Thomson ONE is not so much its conceptual or technological design, but the extent to which the software application delivers tailored and focused information to its clients.

Operational excellence and a performance culture among all the staff supporting the product – articulated in the mantra "performance matters" – are crucial strategic goals. Dunn says:

> Ultimately, the success of Thomson stems from its ability to help our clients increase their own performance using the information and analysis we provide. This, in turn, means we have to increase our own performance – and not just among the staff who have direct contact with the client. Everyone who helps design, deliver and resource our products needs to have the needs of the client in the front of their minds. Only this kind of clarity is going to align everybody behind the task.

Dunn's espousal of mission leadership – and its ability to break down core activities into easy-to-understand and easy-to-measure tasks – was taken in this context. She explains:

> It provided our people with a clear and simple statement of what each individual had to deliver – and why. It provides clarity and a focus on priorities.

An important focus for the introduction of mission leadership was Thomson Financial's concept of "customer touch points", designed to make sure that customer care "from day one" is uppermost in people's minds and informs their behaviour in activities as diverse as product development, information delivery and billing. The way mission leadership has been used to support the touch point strategy illustrates how the concept works in practice. The overall mission – "To significantly improve the customer experience across all Thomson Financial touch points in order to substantiate our 'performance matters' brand positioning" – is broken down into nine sub-missions:

- improve sales experience;

- improve customers' understanding of solutions;
- deliver appropriate desktop support;
- improve customers' "day one" experience;
- develop intuitive and innovative solutions;
- improve the value of content;
- improve customers' experience from ordering to payment;
- make sure that the technology is resilient and reliable;
- improve customers' performance.

Progress against each of these sub-missions is assessed regularly by using the mission leadership dashboard, which has transformed the way Thomson Financial works. It has, for example, revolutionised the way the company develops and introduces new products, making sure that backroom staff (who would normally have little contact with clients) keep customers' needs closely in mind.

Use of the dashboard goes right to the top. Dunn says:

> For our chief executive, the dashboard has become the primary means of reviewing our business performance. It is easy to use and provides updated information. Using it has become part of everybody's normal business cycle. It is always up-to-date and entirely transparent. As a consequence, it enables us all to "stick to it", keeping the main goals and the contribution we make towards them firmly front-of-mind.

The transparency and transferability of mission leadership and dashboard-based performance measurement have also enabled Thomson Financial to tackle the major challenge of integrating disparate working cultures brought about by more than a decade of acquisitions. As soon as they were introduced to its European businesses, Thomson Financial recognised that mission leadership and the mission dashboard could be applied globally, so it introduced them throughout its operations. The initiative was particularly successful in Asia. Dunn says:

> Achieving clarity and alignment, and the change in behaviour that supports this, is a priority anywhere in the world. We have been able to introduce a common performance culture supported by universally applied measurement and review frameworks. Equally important, we have introduced a common language that anyone can sign up to.

How the merger with Reuters will affect this strategy has yet to become clear. (See page 98 for more details of the organisational effect of the merger with Reuters.)

From measurement to leadership

Providing the right milestones and measures is critical to successful strategy execution. Few strategies have been successfully implemented without a wholesale review of an organisation's performance management and financial/business reporting frameworks.

The right measurement framework – whether a strategy map, a balanced scorecard or a dashboard – is important because it will:

- provide objectives that cut across the work of different functions and unify the organisation;
- make sure that the work of all functions (including those of suppliers and partners) is aligned to the strategic goals;
- help senior managers to track performance against long-term plans, making sure that bottlenecks in performance are spotted and addressed quickly;
- target resources where they are most needed;
- make sure that all employees (including those of suppliers and partners) are clear about the contribution they are making towards executing the strategy as well as understanding the roles played by their colleagues and workmates in other departments.

But having the right measures is not enough. The figures have to be interpreted correctly, and the right data will be useless if it is not acted on. Achieving the full benefit of any performance management or business reporting system requires the right leadership.

7 Leadership

Learn from the people
Plan with the people
Begin with what they have
Build on what they know!

Lao-tzu, Chinese sage

What bedevils action is "initiative-itis" – multiple initiatives, often conflicting, rarely completed. In the face of this confusion, line managers are bemused and employees cynical.

Lynda Gratton, professor of management practice, London Business School

Six leadership roles for successful strategy execution

Mark Hurd, chief executive of Hewlett-Packard, becomes suspicious when business leaders are categorised as "visionaries". In Chapter 1, he is quoted arguing that leadership is about getting management essentials right.

His views mirror those of Richard Pascale, a strategy and change management expert at Oxford University. Pascale says that the focus on execution and performance is less on the leader's role as "chief expert" and "chief discoverer" and more on that of "chief facilitator".[1]

But that task is no less important. The strategy needs to be painted in the right context, articulated in a way people will understand as authentic, channelled and focused effectively and supported with the right resources. The most important tasks are:

- instilling focus and clarity;
- generating engagement and commitment;
- allocating scant resources;
- fostering collaboration;
- creating the right milestones of achievement;
- managing pace.

Moreover, these tasks do not apply just to senior managers exercising change from the top. They apply at all levels.

Instilling focus and clarity

The most important task of any manager seeking to execute strategy successfully is to instil the right focus and clarity. Bill Simon's use of the mission leadership technique (see Chapter 3) is a good example. He knows what he is talking about. He came across the principles of mission analysis and leadership during his early days in the US navy and has used them in four different organisations to help them achieve their main strategic goals.

These organisations could not be more different. Using mission leadership techniques, Simon oversaw the transformation of Baileys, Diageo's Irish cream liqueur, from a brand confined principally to the British and American markets to one with genuine global penetration; the extension of the casual dining chains Chili's and Romano's Macaroni Grill into markets as diverse as Latin America and the Middle East; the introduction of commercial efficiencies into the state of Florida's government services; and the foundation of a new health-care and "wellness" business at Wal-Mart. He says:

> *The sector or industry doesn't matter. The principles are the same regardless. It [mission leadership] provides an effective means of generating performance and achieving alignment. It provides you with a cohesive set of targets linked to the main goals of the organisation and helps you engender the mindset needed at all levels of the organisation to achieve them.*

The objectives of the four organisations were achieved using the same basic approach: the establishment of clear goals at all levels of the organisation; the introduction of the right measures to make sure that these goals were being kept on track; and a series of team-based initiatives designed to sign up people at every level by giving them the maximum freedom in how to achieve the mission.

Between 2004 and 2005 Simon was secretary of the Florida Department of Management Services (DMS). One of the tasks he was called on to help fulfil by Jeb Bush, the state's governor, was the "creation of smaller and more efficient government so that better use was made of the taxes paid by Florida's residents".

The mission Simon developed to help meet this goal was to "deliver saving solutions to our customers in order to enable them to better serve the people of Florida". In this case the "customers" were the internal departments served by the DMS. They had the responsibility for achieving goals such as improving student achievement, reducing violent crime and drug use, and helping the most vulnerable. Simon's programme generated substantial cost savings and improved efficiency (see pages 88–9).

He achieved similar success using mission leadership in his subsequent job as senior vice-president, global markets, at Brinker International, which runs branded restaurant chains. His goals were to accelerate growth in the company's strength markets during the 2006 financial year and to lay the foundations for achieving a 20% operating profit by 2010.

He established a series of performance indicators, the most important being to achieve $3.8m in operating profits in 2006 and thus a return on investment of 11%. This was to be underpinned by the opening of 17 new casual dining outlets and developing agreements for 55 further openings during 2007. To achieve these targets, Simon set the mission: "Brinker will be the global casual dining leader by 2010 in order to deliver shareholder value."

To give his senior managers the incentive to achieve this goal, he encouraged them "to explore every opening in the numerous greenfield markets available using unconstrained thinking with the incentive that they had the opportunity to make [company] history". The only constraints were that any opportunities they explored should be within the company's brand guidelines (that is, to build the brand equity of the company's restaurant chains); that their greenfield explorations should aim to be within set targets on financial returns and the restrictions imposed by regulatory reporting; and that any greenfield explorations should also take account of geopolitical (commercial) risks.

Using these guidelines, senior managers took advantage of new contacts in the Middle East to establish two of Brinker's leading casual diner chains – Chili's and Romano's Macaroni Grill – in several countries in the region. In a series of what Simon describes as "flag-planting exercises", 20 outlets were opened in the United Arab Emirates, six in Saudi Arabia and six in Bahrain and Egypt. The groundwork for further openings in Turkey and Lebanon was also undertaken.

Simon points to the successes during his time at Brinker as an example of how mission leadership facilitates innovation as well as underpinning performance:

> It not only provides a structure for achieving the goals of an
> organisation, it also provides frontline staff with the mindset
> to unlock their creative potential. It makes very little difference
> whether the staff involved are government civil servants, brand

managers in the global drinks market, pharmacists or medical
professionals – I've worked with them all.
The sector doesn't matter; it is the process you use to distil
company objectives into missions and sub-missions, the way
these missions and sub-missions are distilled into individual and
team goals, the measures you put into place to enable staff to
monitor their progress against these goals, and the support and
coaching you put in place to give them the skills to do it.

In 2007 Simon took on a new role at Wal-Mart, the world's biggest retailer, which owns supermarkets in several countries including Asda in the UK. Again he is relying on mission leadership to meet the goal he has been set, which is to "lower the cost and increase the accessibility of quality health care". He has encapsulated this role into the mission: "To roll back the cost of quality health and wellness offerings and make them available to 90% of the American population by 2010."

Generating commitment and engagement

Many, even most, large organisations have a history of strategic initiatives that have yielded, at best, mixed results. Almost all the strategies examined in this book were initiated by an incoming chief executive following previous and often poorly executed schemes that generated or reinforced cynicism and apathy. It is also because, regardless of whether previous attempts have been made to tackle the deep-rooted problems that justify the change, the challenges of turning round an organisation in decline and generating commitment to and engagement with change are immense.

Rosabeth Moss Kanter, whose 20-year study of transformational leadership sprang from a background in psychology, argues that corporate decline does not stem from a single factor. It results from an accumulation of decisions, actions and commitments that become entangled in a vicious cycle of secrecy, blame, isolation, avoidance, lack of respect and feelings of helplessness. Once a company is caught in this spiral, it is hard to stop let alone reverse the direction. She concludes:[2]

Organisational pathologies arise and reinforce each other in such
a way that the company enters a kind of death spiral.

Reversing the cycle, using Kanter's formula for success, requires a well-crafted combination of open dialogue, engendering respect, sparking collaboration and inspiring initiative. The tools available to the incoming chief executive – formal consultation programmes, below-the-surface networking using gatekeepers and pulse-takers, the tapping of hidden or latent collaborative groups, the identification and appointment of change champions – have been explored in previous chapters. But the character and perceived integrity of the chief executive and his or her immediate subordinates in the change programme will be crucial.

Paul Levy: winning commitment to the strategy from the outset

When Paul Levy became chief executive of the Beth Israel Deaconness Medical Center in Boston in January 2002, the hospital was losing $50m a year. Relations between the administration and medical staff were strained, as were those between the management and the board of directors. Employees felt demoralised, having witnessed the rapid decline in the hospital's once-legendary status and the disappointing failure of previous change initiatives.

A study had been undertaken by the Hunter Group, a leading health-care consultancy. Its report, detailing the dire conditions at the hospital and the changes needed to turn things round, had been completed but not yet released. Meanwhile, the Massachusetts attorney general, who was responsible for overseeing charitable trusts, had put pressure on the board to sell the failing hospital to a commercial health-care provider.

Levy was convinced that the employees, desperate for change management that actually worked, would co-operate with him if he could emulate and embody the core values of the hospital's culture rather than impose his personal values. He chose to act as the managerial equivalent of a good doctor, one who tells a very sick patient both the bad news and the chances of success honestly and imparts a realistic sense of hope without sugar coating.

Taking his cue from private discussions with the state attorney general, whom he had persuaded to keep the hospital open for the time being, Levy chose to publicise the very real possibility that it would be sold. While he risked frightening the staff and the patients with this bad news, he believed that a wake-up call was necessary to get employees to face reality.

During his first morning on the job, Levy delivered an all-hands-on-deck email to the staff. It opened with the good news, pointing out that the organisation had much to be proud of, but that the threat of sale was very real. Levy signalled the kind of actions employees could expect from him, including job cuts, and described the management style he would adopt. For example, he would manage by walking around, lunching with staff in the cafeteria, having impromptu conversations in the corridors, talking to employees at every opportunity to discover their concerns. He would communicate directly with employees through email rather than through intermediaries. He said the Hunter Group report would be posted on the hospital intranet, where all employees would have the opportunity to review its recommendations and submit comments for a recovery plan.

The direct open tone of the email signalled exactly how Levy's management style would differ from that of his predecessors. It provoked an immediate and positive response. When the Hunter Group report was posted on the intranet two days later, Levy received and personally responded to more than 300 email suggestions in response to its findings, many of which he later included in the turnaround plan.[3]

At the end of the 2004 fiscal year the hospital's financial performance was far ahead of the recovery plan and morale had increased. It made a $37.4m net gain from operations, and the annual turnover of nursing staff, which was 15–16% when Levy took over in 2002, had dropped to 3% by the middle of 2004.

Allocating scant resources

Whether resources – financial, technological or human – are allocated strictly in accordance with the mission and goals set out in the strategy will determine its success. In their book *From Resource Allocation to Strategy*, Joseph Bower and Clark Gilbert of Harvard Business School argue that the cumulative impact of the allocation of resources at any level has more real-world effect on strategy than any plans developed at headquarters. They say:[4]

> *Strategy is crafted, step by step, as managers at all levels of a company – be it a small firm or a large multinational – commit resources to policies, programmes, people and facilities. Because this is true, senior management might consider focusing less attention on thinking through the company's formal strategy and more attention on the processes by which the company allocates resources.*
>
> *Top executives will never be in a position to call all the resource-allocation shots – nor should they be. But they should learn to identify and influence the managers at all levels who can forever alter a company's future.*

Michael Peace, chief executive of Lipper (see Chapter 3), agrees. A clear strategic focus does not just lead to clear job descriptions and clear ownership of each role, he argues. It is vital that the limited resources companies have at their disposal are channelled into the right projects and not frittered away by managers whose activities are not central to the change strategy's main effort.

Planning and allocation of resources in the company has been revolutionised by a cost scorecard launched by Peace. This allows senior managers to balance and prioritise discretionary spending against budget excess or planned savings that can be reallocated to other functions rather than squirrelled away by budget-savvy departments.

Peter Aldridge, chief executive of HSBC Rail (see Chapter 6), also found that effective measurement of performance brought with it a more effective allocation of resources at lower levels of the business. He says:

> We wanted to be serious about putting the right resources into the business. Our strategy dictated that we should make more efficient use of our expertise and our capital, but each business unit wanted different things and the resources to achieve it. When we reviewed our operations, we found that we had more than 60 initiatives across the business. So we took the resources away from the least important and whittled down the number to less than 20.

Creating the right milestones of achievement

Chapter 6 described how the effective use of performance measures not only provides the means to align the activities of business units, teams and individuals with the main goals and missions of a strategy, but also enables each one to focus on the right milestones of progress.

When Bill Simon set the mission of "delivering saving solutions to our customers in order to enable them to better serve the people of Florida" (see pages 83–4), he created a series of goals that served as milestones. These included:

- identifying and implementing state-wide cost savings of $1 billion;
- facilitating the state-wide outsourcing of three government services;
- building a high-performance workforce within all management teams;
- delivering four new innovations across these management functions;
- achieving service improvement of 2% during 2004–05.

To support the achievement of these sub-missions Simon had to set himself a series of goals. He had to provide the right leadership to inspire the necessary commitment among frontline staff; this involved providing appropriate coaching and development so that this commitment was translated into better performance. He also needed to remove the blockages impeding the achievement of this performance, principally by giving staff the authority to operate as needed and providing them with unqualified support.

Before Simon left nearly all these goals had been achieved. Services were delivered more efficiently, with costs reduced by 10% and time savings increased by 5%, and internal customer satisfaction with the services provided by the Department of Management Services increased by more than 15%. Three new innovations were introduced by the department: "My Florida Marketplace", a new procurement system; a fully integrated human resource management system; and a real-estate initiative.

Above all, employee morale and performance were transformed. In 2006 staff turnover was cut in half. Employee satisfaction rates improved by 15%, internal complaints by employees were virtually eliminated over a nine-month period and a new process was put in place so that employees could make their own suggestions on how to improve the workplace or save money.

Fostering collaboration

The missions and goals described throughout this book are almost all designed to cut across specialist functions and give a unifying focus to both an organisation's employees and the myriad suppliers, distributors and other providers working with it.

The "themes" chosen by John Rhodes at Luxfer Gas Cylinders (see Chapter 3) and the goals chosen by Aldridge at HSBC Rail (UK) (see Chapter 6) were selected to provide a focus for collaboration between different and often disparate parts of their organisations. The final stage of the Fast Forward change strategy at Reuters championed by Tom Glocer and John Reid-Dodick – termed "Working Smarter" (see Figure 8.2 on page 98) – calls specifically for collaboration to be instilled in the organisation.

But fostering collaboration is a task with little established good practice to draw on. For this reason, it has attracted the attention of benchmarking groups and academic research departments.

Research in action: The Cooperative Research Advantage Team at London Business School

This project is led by Lynda Gratton (see Chapter 3) and the detailed case work carried out with companies as varied as ABN AMRO, British Telecom, Marriott International and Standard Chartered Bank points to a number of crucial aspects of collaboration that had not previously been understood. The most important are as follows:

- ◪ Co-operation does not arise from a single characteristic. Instead it arises as a result of a whole system of practices, processes, behaviours and norms that together shape a co-operative mindset. Co-operation emerges rather than being built.
- ◪ While practices and processes such as training and rewards can play their part in supporting the co-operative mindset, ultimately co-operation is learned from others. In this learning process, the behaviour of the senior management team plays a crucial role. The London Business School research showed that of all the factors that influenced the co-operative mindset, the co-operative behaviour of the senior team was one of the most influential factors.
- ◪ Conversely, the competitive behaviour among members of the senior team and their assumptions about the competitiveness of others are two of the main reasons co-operation fails to develop and the "big freeze" sets in.
- ◪ Co-operation is fragile. There is a host of attitudes and barriers that can destroy the co-operative mindset and degrade co-operative skills.

In an interview about the findings of her book *Hot Spots: Why Some Companies Buzz With Energy and Innovation – and Others Don't*,[5] Gratton comments:

> *A co-operative mindset arises when a whole system of organisational practices, norms, language, stories and habits are aligned.*
>
> *People are able and willing to co-operate and collaborate, and work gets done better as a result of this. We found over and over again that it was these staring assumptions about how work could be best done that was the starting point to the cycle that leads to deep and skilful co-operation.*
>
> *We discovered that each executive has an individual and idiosyncratic view of how collaboration and co-operation emerged. But beneath this idiosyncratic view, we found executives skilled at building co-operation made four key assumptions:*
>
> *1 **Striving for excellence.** They believed that the energy created by co-operation was not driven by competition between people or groups. Instead, they believed that the key driver of energy was that each*

*individual and each group individually and collectively strived for
excellence. This assumption of excellence was the design principle for
much of the selection, promotion and training within the company.*
2 A sense of mutuality. *If people operated only with regard to their
personal self-interest, then deep co-operation was never possible.
Instead, they went to great pains to help others understand that only
through integrating their interests with those of others would deep
co-operation emerge. It was this sense of mutuality, of a shared rather
than individual destiny, that was crucial.*
3 Co-operation is a behaviour. *While the values of co-operation were
important, ultimately a co-operative mindset was built from co-operative
behaviours. The business then of the executive is to support and
encourage co-operative behaviours so over time they become habitual
ways of behaving.*
4 Being part of a community. *Executives, where there was a
co-operative mindset, acknowledged that we are essentially social beings
and we are fulfilled in our personal and work lives through being part of
a community.*

Managing pace

The final leadership trait most commonly associated with successful strategy execution is the ability to manage pace effectively. This was outlined in the 1990s by Ronald Heifetz, director of the Leadership Education Project at Harvard University's John F. Kennedy School of Government. Instead of defining the problems facing an organisation and then providing solutions, Heifetz argues that leaders should identify the challenges and frame the key questions and issues that the rest of the workforce should grapple with.

Effective leaders free frontline workers from the constraints of unnecessary rules and regulations, challenging current roles but resisting pressure to define new roles quickly. At the same time, they keep the organisation in a constant state of flux by throwing out a stream of new goals or challenges, exposing conflict or letting it emerge rather than continually attempting to restore order.

Heifetz compares the process to regulating a pressure cooker by turning up the heat while simultaneously allowing some of the steam to escape. If the pressure exceeds the cooker's capacity it may blow up, but nothing cooks without some heat.[6]

For example, Reuters' Fast Forward strategy was only one of three inter-locking initiatives taken by the chief executive to restore the fortunes of the company over an eight-year period marked by a dramatic collapse of the company's markets and a plummeting share price. Recognising that the company could not be expected to sustain indefinitely the level of change dictated by the Fast Forward programme, each part was undertaken at a different pace.

The reasons, and how this strategy worked in practice, are outlined in Chapter 8.

8 Change

Dealing with uncertainty should come down to this: employees must respond quickly and creatively to the unexpected and devise counter-moves and initiatives under crisis conditions.

Preston Bottger, professor of leadership and management development, IMD International, Switzerland

Reuters: shifting gear as circumstances demand

There is no more vivid illustration of the self-sustaining and reinforcing nature of change, which can derail the most well-thought-through strategies, than the story of Reuters in the years leading up to its merger with Thomson Financial.

The company has set in train extensive structural change and suffered a major collapse and redefinition of its markets. Its chief executive, Tom Glocer, has presided over not one but three overlapping change management strategies designed to accommodate each wave of change that confronted the company. He explains:

> *Change during this period in Reuters' history has taken place at different paces at different times. Sometimes it has been on our terms, sometimes we have been taken over by events. Change itself has been a constant. The pace has differed, so the ability to shift gears has been at the heart of our strategy.*

First gear: the organisational change programme

The organisational change programme was intended as a classic top-down, 1990s-style corporate restructuring. As an incoming chief executive, Glocer found the company in poor structural shape. Once the market leader in news agency reporting, Reuters was suffering because of the poor performance of subsidiaries such as Instinet and a decline in its terminals business caused by the financial services sector downturn.

The company had become complacent. Competitors were stealing market share, service levels were poor and profits were falling. Glocer says:

> *Over the years the company had grown in a disorganised and unfocused way with a myriad of different systems, products, acquisitions and joint ventures.*

It needed action, and fast.

At the heart of the malaise was an outdated company structure. John Reid-Dodick, the company's global head of human resources for business divisions and the co-designer of the programmes, explains:

> Prior to 2001, the chief executives of the geographical regions had direct ownership and control over most of the sales, marketing, product development, finance, human resources and other resources needed to run their businesses in their regions. This created a multitude of products and services around the world, but it also meant that our organisation was not aligned with how many of our customers were now running their businesses. In effect, the geographic focus of our organisation assumed that an asset manager in Japan had more in common with an investment banker in Japan than with an asset manager in New York.

Therefore, the main focus of the organisational change programme was to restructure the company away from territorial fiefdoms towards delivering a smaller, more focused portfolio of services and products.

Second gear: Fast Forward

As stated in Chapter 4, the organisational change programme was getting into its stride when it was derailed by a sudden collapse in Reuters' markets, brought about in part by the dotcom crisis and a consequent reappraisal of the number and type of database services used by clients. Before the crisis, there was enough elasticity in the market for clients to use competing service providers side-by-side. The crisis forced clients to make choices: to, for example, choose between Reuters and Bloomberg. As Reid Dodick says, "while we retained some contracts, far more than we would have liked went to Bloomberg".

The fall-out led to one of the grimmest periods of retrenchment in Reuters' history.

Glocer's response was to commission an upgraded and expanded version of the organisational change programme, Fast Forward, which had five aims. They were to:

- make Reuters' information indispensable;
- move the business to a single product distribution business structure;
- simplify the product line and reshape the cost base;

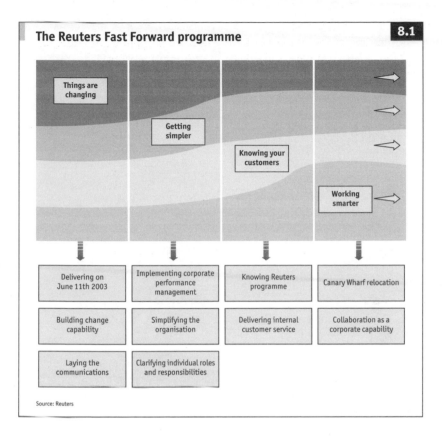

The Reuters Fast Forward programme 8.1

Things are changing	Getting simpler	Knowing your customers	Working smarter

Delivering on June 11th 2003	Implementing corporate performance management	Knowing Reuters programme	Canary Wharf relocation
Building change capability	Simplifying the organisation	Delivering internal customer service	Collaboration as a corporate capability
Laying the communications	Clarifying individual roles and responsibilities		

Source: Reuters

- focus business solutions around the products;
- invigorate the culture and behaviour of Reuters' people.

The resulting Fast Forward transformation programme is shown in Figure 8.1. It is designed to support the restructuring of the company into four global customer segments and to integrate development, infrastructure, content, sales, marketing and other activities into aligned global "centres of excellence" or business services. A human resources focus is the creation of a new culture, based on branded FAST values of being fast, accountable, service-driven and team-focused.

The rationale for the programme was outlined by Glocer in an internal report in early 2004 (see page 39). The crucial difference in the Fast Forward programme was the change in behaviour that it was intended to inculcate in Reuters' employees. The new thrust was to engender the ability to anticipate and respond to continuous change, not just among senior managers but throughout the whole workforce.

Third gear: the Core Plus programme

Fast Forward was designed to make Reuters structurally and culturally better able to respond to the volatile and more demanding markets the company is facing. It was implemented during a period of consolidation and trauma.

The initiative launched by Glocer in 2005, Core Plus, is designed to help the company grow effectively from the roots the Fast Forward programme helped to nurture. The relationship between the two programmes is shown in Figure 8.2 and was outlined in the company's quarterly results in July 2005:

> Reuters' growth prospects are built on a core business reinvigorated by the company's Fast Forward programme. It serves the £6 billion per annum market for financial information and related services, which has an expected long-term growth rate of 2–4%. Through sales of Reuters' desktops and enterprise-wide datafeeds, Reuters expects its core business to grow in line with the market.
>
> Reuters intends to continue to transform its core business after completing Fast Forward to continue to improve time to market, product quality, network resilience and service. New initiatives announced today include concentrating product development into fewer centres; continuing to improve the timeliness and breadth of Reuters' data by streamlining content management; modernising customer administration; and simplifying Reuters' network of data centres. The sale of Radianz to BT Group cut the number of Reuters' data centres from 250 to 160; further simplification is expected to reduce this number to around 10 globally by 2010.
>
> The strategy on which this new initiative is based is expected to deliver:
>
> ◪ three percentage points of revenue growth in 2008, in addition to core revenue growth in line with the market;
> ◪ an incremental £150m of cost savings by 2010, taking total annualised cost savings since 2001 to more than £1 billion;
> ◪ a £1 billion capital return to shareholders, including around £500m from the proposed sale of Instinet Group. Reuters

> *has today put in place an on-market buy-back programme,*
> *which is expected to run for up to two years.*

Glocer, commenting on the announcement of this strategy in July 2005, said:

> *It is a huge step forward for Reuters to see our most closely*
> *watched revenue measure – underlying recurring revenue – back*
> *in positive territory. With Fast Forward nearly complete, Reuters*
> *is healthier, more resilient and poised to deliver stronger revenue*
> *growth.*

As part of the Core Plus initiative, the quarterly results commentary said:

> *Reuters sees four key opportunities for further growth beyond its*
> *core business.*
> 1 *Electronic trading. A significant trend in financial markets*
>   *is that trading is moving from the phone to the screen.*
>   *Reuters is an established provider of electronic trading*
>   *systems – its Dealing 3000 product supports 18,000 dealers*
>   *in interbank (dealer-to-dealer) foreign exchange. As dealer-*
>   *to-customer trading goes electronic, Reuters will launch a*
>   *multi-asset trading platform for markets including fixed*
>   *income, derivatives, commodities and energy. Reuters has*
>   *already started building its presence in these dealer-to-*
>   *customer markets with the launch of four new systems this*
>   *year, including Reuters Trading for Fixed Income. The extra*
>   *investment allows Reuters to accelerate its plans.*
> 2 *High value content. Structural changes in the financial*
>   *markets, including the move to electronic trading and*
>   *restructuring of computer research, are creating demand for*
>   *new types of content. Reuters will introduce new content*
>   *sets that provide context, analysis and insight to supplement*
>   *the news, quotes, company fundamentals and research it*
>   *currently provides.*
> 3 *A new approach to selling content and transactions services to*
>   *whole enterprises. One of Reuters' competitive strengths is the*
>   *relationship it has built with customers over two decades by*
>   *selling enterprise-wide services such as datafeeds and market*

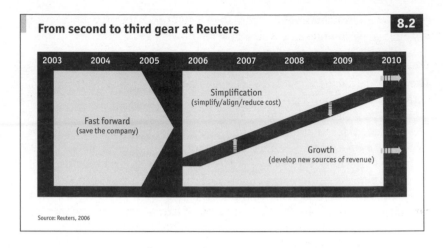

From second to third gear at Reuters   **8.2**

2003   2004   2005   2006   2007   2008   2009   2010

Simplification
(simplify/align/reduce cost)

Fast forward
(save the company)

Growth
(develop new sources of revenue)

Source: Reuters, 2006

data systems. Reuters now plans to market these enterprise capabilities more cohesively and sell suites of components, designed to meet a greater proportion of customers' needs in specific growth areas such as algorithmic trading.

4 *New markets. Reuters plans to increase investment in new markets. It is scaling up its operations in China and India, building an online presence through reuters.com, mobile phones and IPTV [the system that streams video or television programming through a computer] to reach individual investors; and targeting growth in trading of new asset classes such as emissions, weather derivatives and property for further opportunities to launch electronic trading systems.*

Fourth gear: merger with Thomson Group

In spring 2007, the boards of Reuters and Thomson agreed to combine forces using a dual-listed company structure. The companies will be separate legal entities but will be managed and operated as if they were a single enterprise.

Their interests will be aligned and they will pursue common objectives. Thomson will be renamed Thomson-Reuters, and the combined Thomson Financial unit profiled in Chapter 6 and the Reuters' financial and media business profiled above will be called Reuters.

Glocer will be chief executive of the combined business. The merger, on terms highly favourable to Reuters, places a capstone on Glocer's five-year revival of the business and illustrates in great measure the fluctuating fortunes of companies in a turbulent market.

Strategy change management: the new context

The dilemma facing Reuters once the unforeseen collapse of its markets derailed the original goals of a strategy predicated on stable growth is typical of that of many other companies.

In the past decade the causes of change have conflated. The value of seeing change as a once-and-for-all-time tipping point has dissipated as the causes of chaos have multiplied. Technological discontinuities, regulatory upheavals, geopolitical shocks, abrupt shifts in consumer tastes and floods of non-traditional competitors – all these have undermined carefully thought-through change strategies because they are difficult to spot in advance and often hit industries simultaneously rather than in easy-to-control single packets.

Consider the example of Ericsson, a Swedish telecommunications group. In the late 1990s Ericsson was patting itself on the back after successfully completing a five-year pre-emptive change programme led by total quality management and designed to reduce lead times to customers by cutting out redundant processes and (in classic 1990s speak) "moving to a customer-focused, process-based organisation".

Although the strategy was triggered by rapid changes in the telecoms market, the execution of it – which involved commitment-winning, team-building exercises percolated downwards through the group – was conducted on the company's own terms. Lead times were halved and sales costs cut (in some cases by as much as 75%) and Nils Grimsmo, the Norwegian-born chief executive of Ericsson UK, said that he saw "no tendency that [the general rate of improvement] will flatten out. I think we can probably accelerate that improvement".

Within three years, in the same way that the knock-on effects of the bursting of the high-tech bubble in 2001 hit Reuters so hard, Ericsson was crippled by the failure of its mobile handset business and the collapse of capital spending by indebted telecoms operators. The company was in deep trouble. Between 2001 and 2003, it made pre-tax losses of more than SKr64bn (about $9 billion), forcing the incoming chief executive, Carl-Henric Svanberg – the first outsider in more than 60 years to head the company and who had no previous experience of the industry – to slash its workforce by 57,000 and raise SKr30bn (about $4.25 billion) in fresh capital.

The cost-cutting measures taken by Svanberg and his predecessor

Kurt Hellström, together with a heavy investment in third generation mobile telephone technology, turned the company around. But Samberg is not smug about it. Throughout the crisis Ericsson was facing increasing competition from Chinese and other Asian newcomers and this has not gone away. His change strategy is based on maintaining the momentum for change now that the crisis is over:[1]

> There is a constant nervousness. This is not a company
> that is easily complacent. You have to create a bit of a crisis
> environment all the time.

Managing uncertainty: a new management discipline

A new management discipline is emerging: managing uncertainty. As with many emerging disciplines, the boundaries are amorphous. But the disparate concepts and good practice it encompasses can be grouped into three main categories:

- ◪ Managing uncertainty in the commercial environment
- ◪ Managing organisations' response to uncertainty
- ◪ Developing a new kind of leadership

Managing uncertainty in the commercial environment

A leading thinker in this field is Donald Sull, associate professor of management at London Business School, where he teaches a course called "Managing in an unpredictable world". Sull argues that the only way companies can survive the pressures of today's markets is to adapt to changing circumstances in good time and certainly before a crisis hits the business.

That is easy to say but difficult to achieve. Sull argues that it can be done by breaking "adaptation" into three components:

- ◪ **Strategic anticipation.** This is about recognising patterns. Managers must identify early-warning signals from a welter of data, see fresh connections and "find the needles of decisive variables among the haystacks of insignificant ones". They must do this as it happens based on data that are incomplete, ambiguous and often conflicting. They must then select the right mental model to match these circumstances and respond to them.

◪ **Organisational agility.** To succeed consistently in the face of uncertainty, companies need to develop new solutions to novel problems. Adaptation also requires executives to manage a portfolio of internal initiatives to prepare their organisation for opportunities or threats that might arise. Small-scale experiments in new products, services or processes, for example, allow firms to probe how the future might unfold.

◪ **Uncertainty absorption.** Organisations need to place a premium on tactics that absorb uncertainty and build resilience against shocks – good or bad – without trying to anticipate their specific form, magnitude or timing. These include straightforward steps such as lowering fixed costs or increasing operating efficiency. Managers can also diversify geographically while retaining a tight industry focus (as Mittal Steel has done through takeovers), or diversify using a set of resources or competencies (as Royal Bank of Scotland has done through its own sophisticated employee attitude and performance measurement technology which it has used when integrating large companies such as National Westminster Bank).

Sull is keen to avoid the dogmatism that has plagued management theory in the past and so hedges his ideas with caveats. He stresses, for example, that selecting the appropriate mental model to deal with change is fraught with risk and that managers should keep their thinking fluid:[2]

> The tendency to fixate on data that confirm expectations and to ignore non-confirming information leads many executives to hold on to existing ways of thinking for far too long. Part of effective sensing is remaining open to surprises, anomalies and unexpected findings.

This abiding flaw in senior management's ability to determine strategy effectively – picking facts that confirm prejudices rather than dispel them – is explored in more detail by Jerry Wind, professor of marketing at the Wharton School at the University of Pennsylvania, and his collaborator, Colin Crook, a former chief technology officer at Citicorp, a banking group, in their book *The Power of Impossible Thinking*.[3] This outlines a four-point process for senior managers trying to break out of the rigid way of thinking identified by Sull:

◾ **Understanding the power and limits of mental models.** To take advantage of models that shape strategic thinking, you have to know how they shape your sense of possibility and how they limit your ability to anticipate emerging opportunities and threats.

◾ **Testing the relevance of your mental models against changing environments.** As the world changes, do your models still fit? If not, how do you find new models and put together a portfolio of models to meet future challenges?

◾ **Overcoming inhibitors to change by reshaping the infrastructure and thinking of others.** To introduce a new order, Wind and Crook argue, you need to "change the structures of the old world and the thinking of others". You need to bridge different perspectives.

◾ **Transforming your world by acting quickly upon the new models.** By experimenting constantly, you can re-evaluate your thinking, keeping it fresh and relevant and developing ways to apply your insights quickly and effectively using informed intuition.

To illustrate the constraints of old thinking and new mental models, Wind and Crook use the example of the four-minute mile. Until 1954, this feat was thought impossible. Then Roger Bannister broke through the barrier. Within three years, 16 other athletes had also run a mile in less than four minutes. Wind and Crook ask:[4]

> What had happened in those three years? Was there a sudden growth spurt in human evolution? No, the basic human equipment was the same. What changed was the mental model that the limit could be broken and the sense of possibility that this brought with it.

Managing organisations' response to uncertainty

Sull's second imperative – the need to develop organisational agility – is the subject of much detailed research by other academics. The best overview is provided by Jean-Louis Barsoux and Preston Bottger, respectively senior research fellow and professor of leadership and management development at IMD International in Lausanne, Switzerland.

Barsoux and Bottger argue that the idea that managers can analyse their way through the fog of the environment in which they operate is highly dangerous. The reality is that surviving and thriving in periods of uncertainty depends on an organisation developing the right capabilities to generate "fast and powerful responses to environmental volatility". Three capabilities dominate in their thinking:

- **Incisive learning.** Much of the learning that goes on in organisations, they argue, is superficial and not sufficiently incisive because managers at all levels are overconfident, or overstretched or overanxious. Drawing on the work of Wind and Crook, they stress any of these three states of mind is a huge impediment to learning, which, at a deeper level, requires the capacity to develop a fresh perspective. They say:

  It is vital to help executives see connections between emerging signals, to appreciate their significance and to work out responses.

- **The right people.** To build a culture that will deal well with uncertainty, an organisation needs to recruit and develop people with a track record of resourcefulness, who can deal with conflict and whose personalities fit the corporate culture. Barsoux and Bottger say:

  Companies can cultivate these capabilities by exposing high-calibre people to diverse experiences that will help them see things from multiple perspectives.

- **Focus on quality.** This provides a shared language for an organisation's professionals to recognise and debate. It helps people to focus on hard facts and effective actions. It also helps to make sure that bad news quickly works its way through the firm's networks and gets the attention it deserves.

Barsoux and Bottger conclude:[5]

> *Dealing with uncertainty should come down to this. Employees must respond quickly and creatively to the unexpected and devise counter-moves and initiatives under crisis conditions. This means that people at all levels must relentlessly review existing projects and processes and discard those that have lost their relevance.*

Developing a new kind of leadership

Change leadership is hardly a new priority, but the ability to bring clarity to an uncertain and often confusing world is an essential – some would say, the essential – role of a leader. This is the principal argument of Rob Goffee and Gareth Jones, respectively professor of organisational behaviour and fellow at the Centre for Management Development at London Business School.

In their book *Why Should Anyone Be Led By You?*,[6] Goffee and Jones argue that successful leaders must exhibit many qualities but the most important is the ability to observe, understand and react to uncertain situations. This requires three skills:

- **Sensing situations in practice.** This involves a complex mix of cognitive and observational skills that enable effective, intuitive leaders to detect signals and patterns that lesser leaders miss. Goffee and Jones say:

  Effective leaders tune in so that they know when team morale is shaky or when complacency needs challenging. Often they appear to collect this information through osmosis.

- **Rewriting the context.** This consists of behavioural and adaptive skills that enable leaders to work with their followers to "construct an alternative reality". On some occasions this may also involve creating uncertainty for the benefit of the organisation. "In this way the leader translates external pressure into constructive internal pressure."
- **Straight talk.** Effective leaders need to sound and seem authentic. People need to be led by someone real. To attract loyalty and commitment, a leader has to be many things to many people. The trick is to pull that off while remaining true to yourself.

Goffee and Jones take one step further the concepts outlined in the 1990s by Ronald Heifetz. Instead of defining the problems facing an organisation and then providing the solutions, Heifetz argues that leaders should use their "helicopter" perspective to identify the challenges and frame key questions and issues that the rest of the workforce should grapple with. Heifetz also compares the actions a leader needs to take to regulate a pressure cooker by turning up the heat while simultaneously allowing some of the steam to escape. If the pressure exceeds the cooker's capacity it may blow up, but nothing cooks without heat.[7] (See Chapter 7.)

9 Innovation

Perfection can only be accomplished by using old knowledge in new ways.

Robert Sutton, professor of science and technology, Stanford University

East African Breweries: exploring the links between clarity and creativity

The doctrine of successful strategy execution established in Chapter 3 – if people are clear about the goals they need to fulfil and are given the right resources, backing and operational freedoms, this fuels creativity as well as better performance – has been espoused fully by East African Breweries.

The company has long been a leading brewer in the region, with its own Tusker lager brand being the best-selling premium beer in Kenya. But its fortunes have been given a heady boost over the past decade through its partnership with Diageo, which owns a controlling interest in the company. Gerald Mahinda, East African Breweries' chief executive, sits on the Diageo Africa Executive Board and the mission – to become Eastern Africa's leading brewing company by market and segment by 2010 with a more ambitious long-term goal to become the dominant brewer in the whole continent – was tied closely to Diageo's own goal to become the world's leading drinks company.

East African Breweries' goal is simple, but one of the ways it has chosen to achieve it is groundbreaking.

The company has always had a history of innovation throughout its home markets of Kenya, Uganda and Tanzania. It was the first brewer in the region to launch its own lager, Tusker, in 1930. Then in 1996 it launched Citizen, the first beer in the region that used non-malted home-grown barley, itself an innovation in a climate not traditionally appropriate for growing that crop. In 2001 it was one of the first companies in the region to launch a shared services centre to provide co-ordinated support for accounting, human resource management, purchasing and production under a single roof. It has been voted East Africa's most respected company for five years running since 2001.

However, the search for new markets and products to meet the strategic goal agreed with Diageo took East African Breweries into unexplored territory. Two-fifths of beer consumption in Kenya is illicit, based on home brews that are unregulated and often poisonous. To cater for this market, Kenya Breweries, a subsidiary of East African Breweries, launched Senator, a beer specifically targeted at low-income consumers whom the Kenyan government was keen to deter from bootleg brews.

Many of the target group live in slums or shantytowns or in outlying communities not normally accessible to conventional distribution chains. In order to reach these people East African Breweries created its own informal distribution system by setting up micro-financing for budding entrepreneurs to become small-scale local distributors known as "route owners". They move single kegs to local bars on the back of a bicycle.

The initiative has been a great success, aided by tax breaks from the Kenyan government, which sees Senator as a means of tackling the social problems caused by illicit brewing as well as stemming the loss of tax revenues. Mahinda argues:

> It is a win-win situation. The government raises new tax revenues; social issues are resolved; and we develop new production capacity.

The emphasis on creative interpretation of a simple strategic goal – to be the region's leading brewer – is entirely in line with East African Breweries' tradition of searching out new markets and exploring green-field territory through unfettered thinking focused on clear objectives.

Mahinda is also committed to providing his staff with coaching and broader management education to support East African Breweries' growth. Damian McKinney of McKinney Rogers, who was born and bred in Kenya and is a fan of Tusker lager, coaches the company's managers in mission monitoring and managing.

The managers also monitor their progress using PitStop, a measurement system developed in collaboration with McKinney Rogers. Under the system managers conduct "pit stops" every six months, either to set the missions for a new fiscal year or to check that their existing missions are still aligned to the company's main goals. McKinney says this allows teams to "leave charged up ready to drive faster towards the finishing line".

Particular emphasis is placed on coaching senior executives in how to think innovatively. Their leadership skills have been boosted by a session led by John Adair, the UK's leading expert on the subject. Mahinda says:

> All of this enables us to look constantly for new opportunities.

It has helped us seek solutions outside our existing parameters.
That has been its most important contribution to the company.

The underlying need and desire for innovation

Since the 1990s innovation has been recognised as hugely important in giving companies a competitive edge, but in an era dominated by strategic alignment, performance management and the balanced scorecard, innovation management has taken a back seat in academic and management journals. The lack of attention devoted to the subject has puzzled some researchers. As a noted business academic commentator in this field, Gary Hamel commented in an article in the *Harvard Business Review*:[1]

> *Most businesses have a formal methodology for product innovation, and many have research and development groups that explore the frontiers of science. Virtually every organisation on the planet has in recent years worked systematically to reinvent its business processes for the sake of speed and efficiency. How odd, then, that so few companies apply a similar degree of diligence to the kind of innovation that matters most: management innovation.*

Yet fostering management innovation is a crucial result of the strategies pursued by nearly all the organisations profiled in this book. Innovation is a central attribute required by HSBC Rail in its strategic goal "to make the organisation light on its feet". Working innovatively is one of the cross-functional "themes" underpinning the strategy of Luxfer Gas Cylinders. And, as highlighted above, the need for innovation underpins the approach to strategy execution adopted by East African Breweries.

The prevailing thought about innovation and the individual is that instead of focusing on identifying and developing a discrete group of innovative individuals, organisations would do better to create a working environment in which all employees are able and willing to tap their own creative potential. This principle underpins the doctrine of mission leadership (see Chapter 3).

Fostering innovation: eight roles

Much state-of-the-art practice in the past few years has focused on eliminating those aspects of daily work that constrain or inhibit creative thinking and introducing initiatives that foster it. The factors organisations or commentators have focused on most are:

- eliminating blame;
- encouraging people to share their insights;
- recognising and rewarding creative contributions;
- mandating managers to foster new ideas;
- picking the right team leader;
- encouraging creativity in team roles;
- supporting winning ideas with the right resources;
- tapping the organisation's networks.

Eliminating blame

A blame culture affects how people think and what they do. People will not experiment in their work because it carries the risk of failure. They fear the embarrassment and loss of status it brings. Organisations often reinforce this natural tendency when they promote a commitment to "error free" work or announce a "zero tolerance for failure" ethic, as many did under total quality management initiatives in the 1980s.

Undoing the damage is often far harder than doing it in the first place. If managers want their staff to test good ideas at work, they must be explicit in reassuring them that there will be no comeback if anything goes wrong. This was the overwhelming conclusion of a study carried out by Fiona Lee, an associate professor of psychology at the University of Michigan, who with two colleagues at Harvard Business School looked at how hidden assumptions undermined a new initiative at a large American mid-western health-care organisation.[2]

The organisation had recently introduced a website that would give medical staff and administrators a single access point to the most up-to-date clinical information. Because there was no formal training course in using the system, employees had to experiment with it to gain proficiency.

In a survey of 688 staff covering five teaching hospitals, 30 health-care centres and 120 outpatient clinics, Lee and her colleagues assessed how each person used the technology and how this was influenced by the management culture in which they worked. She found that individuals were more willing to experiment with the system – trying out different software applications and testing new features – when their departmental managers explicitly stated that making mistakes was acceptable and did not punish them for making errors.

Managers who gave mixed signals, such as verbally encouraging experimentation while keeping in place a system that punished failure, created mistrust and confusion. The effect of inconsistent messages was particularly strong among junior staff. Medical students, for example, assumed that a failed experiment could harm their careers because of the need to demonstrate their competence to win advancement. By contrast, Lee found employees who were "allowed the room to fail" ended up being the most proficient and satisfied with the new technology as well as being the quickest to integrate it into their everyday work.

The financial cost of failure is another part of the equation. Most manufacturing companies keep a tight control on experimentation because of the research, prototyping and training required to test and refine unproven ideas. The price tag can restrain the willingness of research staff to try out wild ideas that, once in a while, will lead to a breakthrough.

At BMW's research and development centre in Munich a psychological barrier to off-the-wall experimentation with car components is that every prototype requires a new set of tools or models. They are expensive to make and will be scrapped if the experiment is abandoned.

Using moulded plastic that can be sculpted to a high standard of proficiency by laser-design tools, BMW has found a way of reducing the costs of early experiments. Staff feel more free to explore the manufacturing implications of a new component that emerges out of a brainstorming session, for example, because the only significant cost to the company is their time.

Encouraging people to share their insights

People must be willing to share their insights. In the late 1990s Morten Hansen of Harvard Business School combined forces with Bolko von Oetinger, a senior vice-president in the Munich office of the Boston Consulting Group, to promote the need for what they call "T-shaped managers". These are people who share knowledge freely across the organisation (the horizontal part of the "T") while remaining committed to the performance of their own business unit (the vertical part). As Hansen puts it, the successful T-shaped manager must learn to live with, and ultimately thrive within, the tension caused by this dual responsibility.[3]

Hansen's theories are based on work with a number of international organisations that have identified the need for cross-boundary knowledge sharing at a time when organisations are growing less hierarchical and becoming more international and networked through computers.

For example, GlaxoSmithKline, a big pharmaceuticals group, encourages the cross-pollination of ideas through information matchmakers (people formerly mandated to act as networkers) working across different divisions and countries. Siemens, a multinational engineering group, has launched a training programme that puts high-potential managers from different divisions into small teams to solve specific problems raised by individual business units. Ispat, a global steel group, has introduced cross-directorships that require the general manager of every operating unit to sit on the board of at least one other unit.

However, the decision to share insights and knowledge is not simply a matter of managers responding to a new initiative. It is matter of individual choice. Researchers at the Roffey Park Institute in Sussex have identified two ways in which people's willingness to contribute their creativity to the organisation is reduced or negated.

The first is "psychological withdrawal", where uncertainty about their personal future in the organisation through change of any kind leads to fear and stress and, as a consequence, inhibition at work. The second is "psychological work to rule", where more confident staff deliberately hold back their best ideas until they know what personal benefits the change will bring. If the reward does not match their expectations, they use their creative insights to start their own enterprise or secure a better position in a competitor firm.

Whichever happens, the innovative capability of the individual is lost to the firm. Wendy Hirsh and Marion Devine from the Roffey team argue that this is one reason so many mergers fail. The uncertainty surrounding the talks, often communicated to staff only through gossip or press reports, undermines the very capability the merger is designed to exploit. Hirsh and Devine stress that this phenomenon will be countered only if the companies take the time and effort to reassure staff about their future at the start of the process and not, as is so often the case, only once the deal is completed. The same is true of any initiative that, in the eyes of the individuals concerned, will affect their career.[4]

In exactly the same way, the job cuts and promotion freezes that followed the economic slowdown in the latter half of 2001 were either hindered or eased by the level of transparency with which they were implemented. Karen Stephenson's work on the value of "gatekeepers" and "pulse-takers" (see Chapter 4) was inspired during the recession of the early 1990s when such individuals, whose cross-functional positions enable them to communicate with staff across the whole organisation, were used to counter the rumour mill and prevent the loss of creative talent.

Recognising and rewarding creative contributions

The other side of the coin is making individuals feel that it is worth their while to make the creative effort. This can be achieved in a variety of different ways.

One that is common in manufacturing companies is through ideas competitions or reward schemes. Nucor, once a small player in the American steel industry, has helped to transform both itself and the whole industry through the systematic encouragement of innovation. A young engineer working at its Arkansas plant at Blytheville saved the company more than $1m in recurring costs by inventing tapered pieces of metal called shims, which require no lubrication and are therefore cheaper to maintain than the screws supporting steel mill machinery designed for the plant by the manufacturer.

More importantly, engineers at the Crawfordsville plant in Indiana developed a technique called thin-slab casting, which enabled Nucor to compete effectively in flat-rolled steel manufacturing at a fraction of the cost incurred by bigger rivals. In both cases, the breakthroughs were encouraged by an incentive scheme that pays workers a lump sum of up to twice their basic salary for any initiative that boosts productivity.

Other manufacturers report similar breakthroughs. At Kvaerner, a Norwegian shipbuilder, welder Arne Svennson was awarded $38,000 in 1991 for an idea on how to automate the welding of a key component which now saves Kvaerner's subsidiary Kamfab $45,000 a year. Two adjustable rotating welding tables invented by a pair of section managers in another shipbuilding subsidiary have saved the company nearly $5m since 1994. Harald Faru, Kvaerner's vice-president, intellectual property, says:[5]

> *The purpose of all our initiatives is to reach people who would not normally think of putting ideas in a suggestions box and who come up with a stream of ideas in the course of their day-to-day work. While the prize money is always welcome, it is the opportunity to gain public recognition for the originality in the thinking that is the real incentive to take part.*

As part of a modernisation project, the Royal National Orthopaedic Hospital in the UK launched a staff consultation programme backed by a suggestions scheme called "Say So" (if you think so, say so). The managers received valuable feedback on issues as varied as the likely effects on surgical operations of televisual links to other sites and the way in which outpatient care will be transformed by the use of electronic links to support peripatetic clinicians. This feedback has informed and inspired new multi-disciplinary teams which worked with other hospitals to examine the practical implications. Phyllis Shelton, director of business development at the time, said when the "Say So" scheme was launched:[6]

This is an exciting project involving all staff to look critically at what they do and take greater control. It is inspiring what can be done simply by sharing good ideas and by approaching change in bite-sized pieces.

A further way of rewarding inventive staff, given that research by the Massachusetts Institute of Technology suggests that creative people want to follow their own leads, is to support work in which they have a personal stake. Hewlett-Packard allows, and often funds, its scientific staff to travel, take sabbaticals, and even nominate the academic collaborators with whom they would like to work. Going further along the same lines, there is also widespread encouragement to publish scientific papers, take part in international conferences and seminars, and play leading roles in the formulation of industry standards.

Nortel Networks: recognising and rewarding inventors who make a difference

Benchmark studies in the late 1990s suggested to Nortel Networks that it was applying for fewer patents than its main competitors. The company sees the expansion and protection of its intellectual property rights as an essential competitive tool, so it was keen to explore ways in which the challenge of developing, filing and successfully gaining patents could be extended to a broader range of its research and development staff.

Principle
Accordingly Nortel Networks launched its Intellectual Property Awards and Recognition Plan in 1996. The aim was threefold:

- to provide an environment that was conducive to innovation;
- to encourage all research and scientific staff to become actively involved in developing, filing and securing patents for products and technologies developed at its research laboratories and development facilities;
- to raise the level of awareness of the importance of intellectual property as a competitive tool among all staff.

Process
The plan offers both financial awards and public recognition for all employees involved in filing for a patent. There are four grades:

- **Patent filing.** This rewards all inventors involved in the preparation of a patent application when it is filed. The financial reward is paid through the payroll and a framed filing certificate is presented to each inventor where he or she works.
- **Issue of a patent.** This rewards inventors who have had a patent issued. Again, the financial reward is paid through payroll, but also a laser-engraved plaque of the patent is presented to each inventor.
- **Cumulative awards.** These reward inventors who have been involved in a number of patents being issued. Awards are made for 5, 10 and 15 and so on patents being issued.
- **Significant patent awards.** These reward inventors who have been involved in being granted a patent or patents deemed to be of significant value to the company. Examples include patents that have brought in substantial patent-licensing revenue, form the basis of important industry standards, protect one of the company's core technologies or products or have received industry-wide recognition.

Presentations of these awards are made by a senior Nortel manager in the presence of other people granted patents and can take place at sites of scientific or engineering significance. For instance, in the UK such events have taken place at the Royal Greenwich Observatory and at Bletchley Park, where the German Enigma code was cracked during the second world war.

The awards are highlighted in the company's worldwide electronic newsletters and are sometimes reported in external media.

Results
In the years since the plan was launched, the number of invention submissions made by employees has risen significantly, not only in quantity but also in quality. This has led to an increase in the number of patents sought. More Nortel employees now see themselves as inventors and also view their innovations in a business context, thus increasing the number of successful patent applications.

As Richard Epworth, a consultant in technology innovation on Nortel's optical communications programme, stressed in an interview in 2004,[7] the initiative has not so much given a new incentive to Nortel Network's research and development staff, who were already regularly engaged in making patent applications, but to the broader Nortel workforce:

> *As a frequent inventor, I get turned on by the creative process itself and I think the same is true of other regular inventors. The money and the recognition were incidental to the satisfaction we got in breaking new ground. However, the [reward] plan has stimulated and intellectually engaged other employees*

who had not previously considered themselves inventors and has given a much needed boost in recognition of the importance of our work within the organisation as a whole.

Ewan Bewley, the company's director of intellectual property law, Europe, says there has been an important shift in thinking among Nortel Network's line managers:

There was a feeling that the time involved in developing and filing a patent was time the company couldn't afford. The [reward] plan has illustrated that protecting and nurturing our intellectual property is not an incidental activity. It is the life and soul of our future. Winning this recognition alone has made the scheme worthwhile.

Best-practice points
Bewley and Epworth believe that the best-practice points to emerge from the plan are as follows:

- Recognition is as important as reward. The two go together. The "award" validates the "reward".
- Recognition of individuals generates recognition by the organisation. The value demonstrated by senior managers to those involved in successful patent applications has prompted all staff to re-evaluate the importance of intellectual property to the whole company and prompted an increase in the number of active inventors.
- Emphasis should be placed on inventions linked to business imperatives. The greater awareness of intellectual property's impact on the business has generated an improvement in the quality and success of patent applications.

Mandating managers to foster ideas

None of these initiatives would work if managers and supervisors did not take a lead in encouraging individuals to extend their creative boundaries and in championing the results. The author's own research[8] suggests that this is often seen as a discretionary activity, to be indulged in when managers have the time or inclination. For innovation to become part of normal activity, it needs to be an integral part of a manager's role against which he or she is both appraised and rewarded.

Managers can foster the creativity of their staff in any number of ways.

They can act as sponsors, promoting the idea inside the organisation, making sure that it is not dismissed and sustaining interest during prolonged periods of gestation. They can act as sounding boards, allowing the person with the idea to draw on their broader knowledge or impartial viewpoint to inform or validate the premise or to comment on practicalities.

As a member of a project development team or on a one-to-one basis, they can help shape the idea, fleshing out the premise or finding practical ways to make it real. Lastly, they can bring their specialist knowledge to bear – for example, in technology, law or finance – to underpin implementation or to provide a particular perspective.

The transformation of working practices at British Airways through the imaginative design of its Waterside headquarters near Heathrow[9] was the brainchild of its property general manager, Gwilym Rees-Jones. He recognised that a routine relocation to prevent overcrowding could be turned into a heaven-sent opportunity to break down barriers and improve creativity if the building was built with that purpose in mind. He won the board's permission to design the headquarters from scratch, using a layout that would make sure staff from different departments shared the same social facilities and used them for routine meetings.

In all, it took five years for Rees-Jones to get the green light and a further five before the building was opened in 1997. During the critical early years, when the proposal could easily have been dismissed as an expensive pipe dream – the final cost was £200m – Rees-Jones received support from both inside and outside the company.

The first step was to find vacant land on which to build the headquarters. The then chief executive, Sir Colin Marshall, insisted that the new building must be at or near Heathrow. The only site available was derelict and at the north-western perimeter of the airport. Although it had been used as waste tip by the construction company that owned it, it was still designated a greenfield site by the local authority.

Residents were suspicious of a further imposition on their privacy by BA and raised strong objections to the site being used for commercial purposes. Most of the board, including Robert Ayling, Marshall's prospective successor, who later championed the project, wrote off any prospect of obtaining planning permission. The proposal would have been dismissed there and then had not Rees-Jones received the unexpected support of Gordon Dunlop, the company finance officer, who argued that the land was being sold cheaply and was a good investment in its own right. Dunlop continued to sponsor the proposal for two years, making sure that it was aired at regular intervals.

The next step was to produce a design that would meet Rees-Jones's objectives. In this, he was helped by two sources of expertise. In thinking through the relationship between working environment and creative interactions, he drew on the work of Tadeusz Grajewski and Bill Hillier of the UK's Bartlett School of Architecture. A report, *The Social Potential of Buildings*,[10] gave Rees-Jones the knowledge he needed to draw up the right architectural proposal and they acted as advisers when he created a business plan to put to the board.

Rees-Jones's proposals remained theory until he found an architect who could turn them into reality. That person was Niels Torp, a little-known Norwegian who had designed the SAS headquarters in Stockholm and whose background in town planning made him sensitive to the role of human behaviour in designing buildings. Torp's designs envisaged six self-contained business units connected to each other by "The Street", a 175-metre long tree-lined boulevard containing a newsagent, bank, travel office, florist, supermarket, restaurant and a health and beauty salon. Floors on different levels are connected by walkways containing sofas, easy chairs and coffee tables, providing easily accessible points for casual encounters.

The flow of staff from different parts of the building is carefully chan-nelled to make sure the communal areas are used to the maximum. It is not possible, for example, for employees to go directly from the underground car park to their offices; they can only get to them via The Street. Torp's design incorporated a 200-acre park containing lakes and waterways to surround the building. This is open to the public – which helped enormously in BA's gaining the planning permission it needed for the project to proceed.

Rees-Jones now had the site, the architectural designs and planning permission. All he needed was the board's permission to go ahead. The financial plan he proposed to lay before the directors was based on the initial investment of £200m being offset by demonstrable savings of £11.5m a year by moving from other leased sites and the money BA would save by not having to upgrade them periodically. He also estimated that £3.5m would be saved each year through an annual 2% rise in productivity generated by improved creativity and motivation (this was achieved in the short term).

It was a difficult case to make. The most controversial element – the £3.5m annual saving – was based on a hypothesis that could not be demonstrated on paper. Rees-Jones was greatly helped by rehearsing his presentation in front of the retiring chairman, Lord King, who was sceptical about the plan. Rees-Jones won him round, and the boost this gave to his confidence combined with refinements he made to the presentation helped him win the board's approval.

Rees-Jones's five-year campaign to build Waterside shows that it is not enough for a single person, however creative, to come up with an idea that will make a difference. He or she needs the support of a variety of individuals who may have to stick their necks out to turn the concept into reality. If managers do not see such encouragement as part of their role, the opportunity for their organisations to fully exploit the creativity of their workforce becomes a lottery dependent on having the right person in the right place at the right time.

Picking the right team leader

That puts much pressure on the team manager or project leader. Commentators such as Dorothy Leonard, professor of business administration at Harvard Business School, and Anthony Jay, a former BBC producer and scriptwriter of, for example, *Yes Minister* and *Yes Prime Minister*, who has some involvement in business thinking, see them as the pivot of the creative process. Jay says:[11]

> *If a creative leader is removed from a group, it becomes an extinct volcano. If a firm wants to weaken a competitor, one of the cheapest and most effective ways is to identify the creative groups and offer the leaders lucrative and attractive jobs on its own staff. It is not important that it should need them itself, although they ought to prove an invaluable addition to the strength, only that the competitor should be deprived of them.*

Why? As Leonard stresses, team leaders in a project-based organisation have direct control over almost everything that will determine whether the result is genuinely creative or a damp squib.

They influence or appoint the team members, drawing on memory to select the right balance of lateral thinkers, specialists and shapers – often choosing people who have been sidelined in their careers and have something to prove. They protect loners, making sure that their lack of team or social skills does not result in their contribution being dismissed or marginalised. They shield the team from unrealistic expectations, negotiating the time and resources it needs to fulfil its remit.

Above all, they determine how the group works. As the remit of teams has moved from finding the best way of fulfilling a set task to generating original ideas, a great deal of constructive attention has been focused on the way ideas are inspired and shaped collectively – and traditional methods have been found wanting. Tom Kelley of IDEO, an American design company, says:

> The trouble with brainstorming is that everybody thinks they already do it. Their eyes glaze over when I mention that brainstorming is an art, more like playing the piano than tying your shoelaces, because they equate brainstorming with being no more than an animated meeting.

Kelley's criticisms of brainstorming as it is often conducted in meetings are similar to those made by psychologists over the past three decades, including Alex Osborne, Edward de Bono and Tudor Rickard. Rigid thinking shuts out wild ideas that, while they might be unworkable, get participants to think originally.

The tendency for both the originators of ideas and their critics to analyse any new suggestion to death when it is barely out of the mouth cuts off the flow of original thought. There is nearly always a lack of understanding among participants and organisers that what counts in a brainstorming session is not the quality of ideas but their volume, because the energy this creates moves people's thinking on.

Kelley's own company, founded by his brother David in 1978 and based in California, has been responsible for a diverse range of products, from the Polaroid I-Zone camera to Crest Toothpaste's Neat Squeeze tube.

At IDEO, brainstorming "the right way" is the principal way of tapping collective thought. Design teams are expected to make mistakes early and often. Coming to a "right" solution too quickly is discouraged. People are encouraged to question any and all assumptions and are not regarded as innovative unless they are challenging the client's, the team's and their own pre-existing notions.

Conference rooms have brainstorming rules such as "Encourage wild ideas" and "Be visual" stencilled on the walls in six-inch high letters. Rather than using the emerging digital technologies to collect ideas, low-tech tools such as markers, giant Post-It notes and rolls of paper on tables are used to better effect.

Sketching, diagrams, mapping sequential trains of thought and primitive illustrations such as stick figures are physical tools that enable facilitators to capture the ideas and keep pace with the energy of the discussion. Thus the basic traps of brainstorming are avoided. These include letting the boss go first (he or she will set the agenda and boundaries, immediately

Table 9.1 **Five key roles in ideas development**

Role	Definition	Often undertaken by
Spark	The person who sparks the creative process by spotting or coming up with the idea, creating the vision or defining the need	Anyone employed by or associated with the organisation; often comes from the least expected area
Sponsors	The people who promote the idea or project inside the organisation, making sure that it is not dismissed, and who sustain interest during difficult or lean times	Senior line managers, members of the board, non-executive directors
Shapers	The people who make the idea or project "real", using their own creativity to flesh out the premise and/or find practical means to achieve the objective	Members of the project team appointed to implement the idea, process-oriented consultants, R&D staff from suppliers
Sounding boards	People outside the project whose objectivity and broader knowledge can be drawn on to inform and validate the premise or to comment on the practicalities	Informal or formal members of personal or professional networks, trusted colleagues or company-appointed mentors, strategy-oriented consultants, academics or researchers in the field
Specialists	People who draw on their specialist skills to shape the idea or project from a specific standpoint and use the opportunity to break new ground in the field	Members of the project team, consultants (process and strategy), academics and researchers, R&D staff from key suppliers

Source: Roffey Park Institute, 2000

limiting the brainstorm), taking turns (democratic, painless and pointless, according to Kelley) and relying on the contribution of experts who may have the right knowledge but not the perspective or insight to see beyond it.[12]

Encouraging creativity in team roles

Building on the work of team discussions are contributions from an array of people who have an equal role to play in turning an idea into a commercial proposition. The author's own research[13] suggests that as well as the people directly involved in shaping breakthroughs in thinking or insight, a number of other equally important roles need to be in place.

The most important roles team members can play in shaping and building on new ideas are set out in Table 9.1. They include the following:

- Sponsors – the people who promote the idea inside the organisation, making sure that it is not dismissed at birth and sustaining interest in it during the prolonged period of gestation.
- Sounding boards – people outside the project whose objectivity and broader knowledge can be drawn on to inform or validate the premise or to comment on practicalities.
- Specialists – people who draw on expert knowledge or skills to shape the idea from a specific standpoint, often using the opportunity to break new ground in their own field.

These roles are often best played by managers or specialists who are outside the organisation or on its periphery because they can step back and frame the concept or idea on a broader canvas.

Royal National Orthopaedic Hospital: fostering innovation through creative team roles

Creating the right team roles to enable specialist medical consultants and professional managers to work effectively together was a strategic priority for the UK's Royal National Orthopaedic Hospital (RNOH) between 2000 and 2003.

As with all state-run healthcare providers, the RNOH was organised into a "trust" with the roles of specialist medical consultants (who provide the healthcare expertise) and professional trust managers (who oversee functions such as finance and human resource management) carefully delineated. As in many trusts operating in the UK, this resulted in disruptive tensions between the consultants and the trust managers which disrupted and undermined healthcare projects central to the trust's remit.

The context

The context of the innovation in team roles was a £20m project to refurbish and re-equip the trust's main hospital campus in Stanmore, Middlesex. As well as the basic refurbishment of operating theatres and an increase in bed capacity, the aim was to provide the RNOH with the means to train the National Health Service (NHS) workforce more widely in the latest innovations in orthopaedic care, working closely with a new professor of orthopaedics at the University of London's Institute of Orthopaedic and Musculoskeletal Science.

One aim of the trust's programme of clinical innovation was to revolutionise the delivery of orthopaedic procedures. The strategy drawn up in autumn 2000 committed the RNOH to the delivery of outpatient services flexibly through telemedicine, telephone and picture archiving and communication systems (PACS) links, the introduction of smart technology in theatres and the development of partnerships that extend access to the RNOH's specialist services. (PACS enables images such as x-rays and scans to be stored electronically and viewed on screens.)

Three projects in particular spearheaded the drive to meet the trust's targets. Between 2000 and 2002, the RNOH opened two voice-activated endosuite facilities. These automated systems built into an operating theatre improve productivity and allow live operations to be used for training. These facilities, the first to be incorporated into a hospital theatre in the UK, were closely linked to a new telemedicine suite which allows consultants and students from different hospitals to view a patient's treatment using a television link, greatly enhancing professional training and education.

In parallel with these site-based facilities, the RNOH has designed and launched a range of interactive CD-ROM products including one on primary hip replacement, the first of its kind in the field of orthopaedic surgery. Aimed at general practitioners and orthopaedic surgeons throughout the world and using state-of-the-art animation, the CD-ROM covers all aspects of total hip arthroplasty, from a patient's first visit to the outpatient clinic through the pre-operative planning phase to the surgical procedure itself.

The underlying concept

As executive director for corporate development during this period, Phyllis Shelton's most important role in executing the strategy was to support the programme of clinical innovation that accompanied the refurbishment. By examining previous innovative breakthroughs at the RNOH, she identified three roles involved in all successful projects:

◪ A clinical champion – someone responsible for spotting and championing the innovation and ensuring that its main aims cut a seam through the whole project. This is often, but not necessarily, a clinician.

- ◪ A shaper – someone responsible for placing the project innovation in a wider strategic context and who acts as a "gatekeeper" for the necessary trust backing and resources. This is usually a trust manager with a broad-ranging business development remit.
- ◪ An implementer – someone with the right teamworking and leadership skills who can put together an effective project team of internal clinicians and trust managers, external suppliers and specialists, working to a remit provided by the innovator/champion and the shaper, and making sure that the external suppliers work to it too.

The concept in practice
Shelton observed that a project with a champion, shaper and implementer usually succeeded, but if any of those roles were lacking it usually failed. She therefore pioneered the role of trust manager as both "shaper" and "implementer" and clinical consultants as "champions". Her own partnership with the clinical consultant acting as innovator in the CD-ROM initiative illustrates the balance of roles.

As the designer of most of the RNOH's postgraduate surgical courses, the consultant had long identified the need for interactive tuition and the potential of CD-ROM technology to foster it. Shelton supported the consultant in choosing and liaising with the right suppliers, winning the necessary sponsorship, undertaking internal research among consultant practitioners, overseeing the launch and encouraging post-launch take-up.

Without the consultant, the inspiration behind the project would not have emerged. Without her role as the corporate development manager, it would not have happened. They had a joint commitment to the project, and the skills they brought to it were radically different but mutually dependent.

The choice of lead supplier is a good example. Primal Pictures, the company chosen to undertake the production work, has built up a reputation as a new breed of medical education company. It created the world's first complete 3D computer graphic model of the human body which has a level of detail, clarity and functionality that is, according to the consultant on the project, "beyond anything to date".

The consultant provided the specialist expertise that enabled Primal Pictures to provide 3D animations of the instruments used and the procedures alongside explanatory texts and a detailed reproduction of the Stanmore hip, the gold-standard prosthesis developed by the RNOH in the early 1960s and now manufactured by BioMork. But it was Shelton as corporate development manager who identified Primal Pictures as the ideal partner. She also drew up the specification, oversaw the quality assurance process, negotiated with sponsors and obtained a series of testimonials from orthopaedic surgeons.

In another initiative – the development of cartilage transplantation as a groundbreaking surgical technique in the repair of cartilage damage – sustaining the project involved winning the support of the trust's board for a programme of trials and backroom work. This lasted for years and significantly affected the day-to-day activities of the consultants championing the procedure.

The procedure uses cell culturing to create a covering membrane. This reduces the time spent undergoing surgery and spares the patient long and painful follow-on treatment, particularly in the case of knee injury. Originally developed in Sweden, it has been launched and piloted in this country by the RNOH in conjunction with Verigen, a biotech company.

In this case, Shelton – acting as shaper – was responsible for putting together and gaining the backing of the trust for the trial procedures, including a pilot project on a private patient, regular contract review meetings and supporting health economics studies. At key stages of trial process – particularly the successful review of the procedure by the National Institute for Clinical Excellence (NICE) in 2000 – she was the arbiter between the professional agenda of the practitioners and the (sometimes overtly) commercial interests of the supplier.

Working with consultants, who acted as clinical innovators, she was also responsible for developing and overseeing a national study to support the NICE review. This entailed:

- training all the UK surgeons in the technique;
- establishing and maintaining a database of patients;
- establishing a UK-wide clinical network for cartilage transplantation where staff at 25 centres around the country are trained and supported to deliver the service and submit all their data to the RNOH for review;
- supporting NHS business managers and therapists through regular network meetings.

The added value provided by Shelton in these initiatives was not simply micro-level management and project co-ordination skills; it was willingness and the ability to champion outcomes that she saw as having strategic importance for the trust. In the case of the CD-ROM project, for example, the immediate revenue it generated was minimal. It was costly to produce, time consuming and added little to the balance sheet.

Shelton's willingness to devote large amounts of management time to the project – including post-launch attempts to foster practitioner take-up that she thought should be undertaken by what she terms "clinical champions" – was not based on agreed job-specific priorities. Indeed, there is nothing in her job specification that mandates her to foster innovation at the trust, particularly if the effort involved conflicts with more immediate clinical or trust-related priorities.

And there lies the rub, in her eyes. Her dedication to fostering innovation at the RNOH, when she was working for the trust as an executive director, was discretionary. If her successors do not share her enthusiasm, there is nothing to oblige them to take up projects like the cartilage transplant or the CD-ROM, both of which, like most gestating innovative initiatives, are hard to justify in terms of hard accounting criteria.

Sustaining innovation of this kind, at a time when attention is focused on immediate delivery in a service that is profoundly change-weary, means embedding the process into day-to-day management tasks. Facilitating the development of ideas should, in Shelton's view, form part of a trust manager's job specification and annual performance targets should be set, measured and reviewed in annual appraisals.

Supporting winning ideas with the right resources

Once the development of an idea has reached a certain point, a decision must be made whether to back it with sufficient resources or write it off. Pharmaceuticals companies, for example, depend largely on internal investment decisions about which research projects to support and which to abandon.

GlaxoSmithKline claims that its ability to sustain a steady stream of new products is the result not just of luck and investment but also of swiftly killing projects that seem unlikely to yield results in favour of searching for new uses for existing drugs. For example, Lamivudine, a treatment for hepatitis launched in 1996, is essentially a lower-dose version of 3TC, one of the firm's AIDS treatments.

The company's effectiveness in making these decisions was boosted in the early 1990s by reforms introduced by an impromptu partnership of managers working for the then SmithKline Beecham: Paul Sharpe, director of project management in neuroscience at the company's Harlow plant in the UK, and Tom Keelin of the Strategic Decisions Group, an international management consulting firm based in Menlo Park, California.[14]

Sharpe and Keelin reviewed the way in which investment decisions about core research and development projects were made, and did not like what they found. In some cases, decisions to favour one project rather than another were made by little more than a show of hands. In others, projects were scored using seemingly objective criteria such as commercial potential, technical risk and investment requirements. But the information underpinning these criteria was provided almost entirely by project champions who stood to win or lose all from the decisions, since little attempt was made to draw any lessons or useful insights from projects that were terminated.

To increase transparency in the process, the two managers developed a new decision-making framework. Each project team competing for investment had to brainstorm, under controlled conditions, how they would respond if they won:

- the funding they were looking for;
- less funding;
- more funding;
- no funding but were asked to salvage what they could from what they had already achieved.

The company gained significant benefits from this new approach. First, it got teams to start their discussions from the standpoint that this was not a win all/lose all situation. Projects that would have been eliminated under the previous all-or-nothing approach were given a chance of survival. Project champions were also less inclined to exaggerate or distort the claims or statistics on which the decision would be made.

Second, the cross-team synergy that resulted from the brainstorming created a fresh pool of ideas that would otherwise have been lost and that were often applicable to other projects. The requirement for a team to consider what aspects of their project could be salvaged in the event of a failed bid created a win-win situation because the losers gained as much credit for their work as the winners because their ideas could be adapted for other projects.

Identifying which business ideas have real commercial value is one of the most difficult challenges any organisation faces. Not unsurprisingly, a number of business school academics have developed models for the wise investment of resources.

W. Chan Kim and Renée Mauborgne at INSEAD in Fontainebleau, France, have developed six "utility levers" to test the market viability of new ideas:[15]

- **Customer productivity.** What is the biggest block to customer productivity? How does the innovative product or service eliminate it?

- **Simplicity.** What is the greatest source of complexity customers face? How does the innovation dramatically simplify this?
- **Convenience.** What is the greatest inconvenience customers encounter? How does the innovation remove it?
- **Risk.** What are the greatest uncertainties customers face? How does the innovation eliminate these risks?
- **Fun and image.** What are the biggest blocks to fun and image? How does the innovation add emotion or cachet?
- **Environmental friendliness.** What causes the greatest harm to the environment? How does the innovation reduce or eliminate this?

Kim and Mauborgne also stress that taking the right decision about who you work with is critical to the successful exploitation of any new concept. Many innovators try to carry out all the production and distribution themselves, they argue, with disastrous results. No one organisation has all the capabilities required, and unless the new product is extremely well protected by patents or intellectual copyright, time works against the innovator in favour of the imitator.

Tapping the organisation's networks

Chapter 4 showed how the social analysis of an organisation's networks – as championed by Karen Stephenson – helped senior managers keep in touch with the feelings and attitudes of staff on the ground during the early communication and consultation phases of executing a strategy.

Dedicated social network analysis is also important if an organisation is trying to foster innovation as a significant output of a strategy. In an interview with the author, Stephenson looked at how this has benefited Hewlett-Packard, one of the companies she has worked with closely (see box).

How social network analysis benefited Hewlett-Packard

Very few organisations begin their life as a network. Most start out as well formed hierarchies. Rare are the companies that begin their life as a network. Hewlett-Packard is one such company. Its founders walked around to visit each and every employee when the company was small, not just to know their names but to take a personal interest in their life and work. After a while, an overwhelming sense of trust pervaded the company and by the sheer example set by the leaders, the rank and file walked about, getting to know everyone else as well. It was a contagious practice.

Even after the company grew to a considerably larger size, the founders and employees maintained this management style and walked about. So powerful became this legacy that in every business school, a case is taught on "management by walking around" fondly named after the HP founders' guiding management principles.

If you begin your professional life by trusting your professional colleagues in complex, interwoven networks, then the result will be a highly innovative company and a highly motivated workforce – a workforce that would be entirely unprepared for what would be the hierarchical management style of the newly installed chief executive, Carly Fiorina, as well as the hierarchical culture of its merger-mate, Compaq computers, a year or so after Fiorina became chief executive.

Fiorina surrounded herself with a band of highly trusted insiders and rarely, if ever, did she leave the executive suite or put down the executive crown to walk around. While employees knew Fiorina had a virtual open door through which they could email their suggestions about the future of their company, the virtual mode of communication was a weak substitute for the past-felt reality of a personal relationship with leadership. The company was big, but not that big, and Fiorina could have made a significantly symbolic gesture and walked about, if only to alleviate the initial concerns of the employees, a move she never made.

Increasing cultural malaise was exacerbated by the controversial 2002 merger with Compaq which although it got off to a good start, was by late 2003 mired in worries about how Hewlett-Packard was falling increasingly behind competitors such as Dell and IBM, and that it needed a chief executive with more operations expertise. Not much more than a year later, in February 2005, Fiorina stepped down at the board's request and a humble engineer, Mark Hurd, the kind of person who was trained to walk about, walked into the leadership role (see Chapter 1).

Look below the surface

Innovation is linked directly with successful strategy execution because there are always people out there breaking new ground or doing things in a radical way but whose isolated successes are rarely captured, codified and transferred into the mainstream in a way that is linked directly to the strategic goals and missions.

As Richard Pascale, the author of numerous books and article on transformational change in the 1990s, says:[16]

> Ordinary change management methods do not do a very
> good job of bringing "positive deviants" into the mainstream.

> *Managers either overlook the isolated successes under their noses or, having spotted them, repackage the discoveries as templates and disseminate them from the top. This seldom generates the enthusiasm necessary to create change.*

It is crucial, Pascale argues, to "engage the members of the community you want to change in the process of discovery, making them the evangelists of their own conversion experience". In other words, look below the surface to find the creativity that will make the change real – and give the originators credit for it.

Goldman Sachs: bringing organisational deviants to the surface in a way that supports strategy

In 1999, Goldman Sachs' Private Wealth Management business unit in the United States had had several initiatives imposed from the top that senior managers felt had failed to achieve the pace of change needed for the unit to stay in step with the marketplace. It was about to have yet another foisted upon it. Its field-force of more than 300 investment advisers was under strong pressure to adopt an unproven business structure imposed by what one of them described as "our New York headquarters' far-reaching hand".

Investment advisers in the field historically operated independently or as teams of two. Each unit evolved highly idiosyncratic approaches to the work of persuading high-net-worth clients to entrust it to manage their money. Success depended on an investment adviser's ability to create deep, trusting relationships with clients that often lasted for generations. As part of these relationships, clients often invited their investment adviser to weddings, bar mitzvahs and graduations, extending the relationships to their heirs.

By late 2000, the Private Wealth Management division's senior managers were concerned that the industry was undergoing a seismic transformation. Investment firms were under pressure to deliver greater transparency and accept extra regulatory compliance while simultaneously reducing their brokerage fees.

A battle between the unit and its New York headquarters over how the company should respond to this change ensued. Both agreed that the issue Goldman Sachs had to confront was how the company could retain its clients, improve its profitability and grow its assets in a depressed but increasingly competitive environment. New York's solution was to transfer the investment advisers' approach from a model that relied heavily on brokerage income to one focused on fee-based advice, but the unit's frontline staff felt that the change did not suit them and adopted the maxim "If it ain't broke, don't fix it".

A senior manager of the units at the centre of the dispute broke the impasse by asking his investment advisers directly: "Are some teams, with similar territories and prospects, able to thrive in this difficult climate?"

To find out, a six-person council of influential advisers (selected as "guerrilla" leaders from the national network of offices) spearheaded a salesforce effectiveness inquiry. Its members assured the rank and file that any findings would be tested for relevance and "scalability" – what worked for the best team in Boston, for instance, would also have to work just as well for teams elsewhere.

Phase one of the project began in 2000 with a two-month discovery period that identified five practices that marked out the work of the most successful teams. Phase two expanded the process by creating a "roll-out squad" (also made up of the most laterally minded teams) for each practice to test its transferability.

The squads then spearheaded the introduction of each practice throughout the network of offices, visiting each site and explaining why and how the particular practice worked. There was one person from each squad in each office, so one of the presenting investment professionals could double as a local expert on the topic. When local teams had questions, they turned to this representative of the squad.

The result was that all the investment advisers felt that the change was based on practices they had pioneered, not the preconceptions and one-size-fits-all approach adopted by the New York headquarters. Old rivalries between the teams also subsided.

As a result, the Personal Wealth Management unit has been transformed from a marginal profit producer to a major contributor to Goldman Sachs' earnings. The average productivity of advisers has nearly doubled. In these circumstances, the fee-based model so fiercely resisted by the unit at the start has been almost universally accepted and the assets of high-net-worth people being managed by Goldman Sachs has topped $130 billion.[17]

10 Pathway

Bridging the gap between what is happening and what is possible is what change management is all about.

Richard Pascale, author, *Managing on the Edge* and *Surfing on the Edge of Chaos*

A pathway to successful strategy execution

This chapter distils the lessons from previous chapters into a pathway for managing the execution of any strategy effectively (see Figure 10.1 overleaf). It is predicated on the idea that successful strategy execution depends on two factors:

- A focus on the right strategic goals, led and championed by senior managers, that unites an organisation behind the strategy, determines the measures and milestones of success and makes sure that resources – financial, technological and human – are allocated effectively.
- The freedom granted to all parts of the organisation – individuals, teams, suppliers and strategic partners – to be creative in finding new and innovative ways of carrying out these goals.

The role of the leader in providing a proper focus

The role of effective change leaders is described in Chapter 7. It requires managers at all levels to:

- generate engagement and commitment to the required change;
- impose focus and clarity, pinpointing priorities and making sure they are adhered to;
- allocate scant resources to make sure this takes place;
- foster innovation by encouraging and supporting the ideas and changing the working practices of everyone within the organisation;
- create the right milestones of achievement by using measures that show effectively how far the organisation has progressed;
- manage the pace of change by shifting gear according to how much stress the organisation can bear;

Pathway to successful strategy execution `10.1`

FOCUS

SUCCESSFUL STRATEGY EXECUTION

Anticipate the likely CHANGE that will impact on the strategy and ensure that strategic goals are adjusted and updated (see Chapter 8)

Foster a culture of INNOVATION to allow business units, teams and individuals the freedom to fulfil their objectives creatively (see Chapter 5)

Review performance against targets regularly to ensure the effective ALIGNMENT of business units, teams and individuals to key strategic goals (see Chapter 6)

Introduce new MEASUREMENT systems to provide the right milestones of achievement (see Chapter 6)

Identify the BEHAVIOUR needed to fulfil these objectives and inculcate these using coaching and other personal support (see Chapter 5)

Support the introduction of these objectives with the right COMMUNICATION and consultation (see Chapter 4)

Break key goals into business unit, team and individual objectives to create CLARITY of role

Create the right FOCUS, using cross-functional theses to unite the whole organisation

FREEDOM

Source: Midel Syrett 2007

◪ sustain the process by constantly reassessing the organisation's internal needs and anticipating the likely onset of further change triggered by outside circumstances.

The focus of strategy leadership relies less on the leader's role as chief expert and chief discoverer and more on that of chief facilitator. The language of modern leadership – help, clarify, orient, frame – presupposes that the impetus for change and innovation is already in place and needs driving effectively. In the amoebic process of transformation, the organisation is already in constant motion. The leader provides the impetus and the pace.

The freedom given to the organisation to respond creatively
The capabilities required to respond effectively to the right leadership are described in Chapter 9. An organisation should be:

- **transparent** – letting everyone see everyone else's real work and letting people filter and sort for themselves;
- **engaging** – aiming to actively involve employees not only in implementing the strategy but also in shaping it;
- **collaborative** – building trust between people in the organisation and between organisations;
- **disruptive (and deviant)** – flushing out the rebels who thrive on disruption and nonconformity and making them the organisation's best agents of change;
- **well-networked** – enabling a free flow of ideas between work units and allowing centres of best practice to emerge and share their work;
- **amoebic** – adapting and shifting in line with change below the surface.

To support this capability, an organisation needs the right measures of progress and milestones. These are described in Chapter 6. The workforce will also require the right training and organisational learning initiatives linked directly to the overall aims and key goals of the strategy. Examples are described in Chapter 5.

The interdependence of the right focus and organisation's freedom to respond creatively

The two requirements for successful strategy execution – the right focus and the ability of an organisation to respond creatively – are mutually dependent. The reason is illustrated in Figure 10.2.

If an organisation benefits from the right focus but does not have the capacity to respond creatively, the execution of a strategy will be undermined by a lack of responsibility for it among the workforce, a lack of collaboration between essential work units or strategic partners and friction at middle or junior management levels.

By contrast, if an organisation already has the right creative freedoms but the direction provided by senior executives – in terms of overall strategy, stated goals and priorities, measures and milestones or the right pace – is misplaced, its ability to respond will be undermined by a failure to see the bigger picture, uneven progress, little focus of energy and effort and poor resource allocation.

Only when effective leadership is supported by a change management capability throughout the organisation will it achieve focused performance, total commitment to and responsibility for the solution, and the

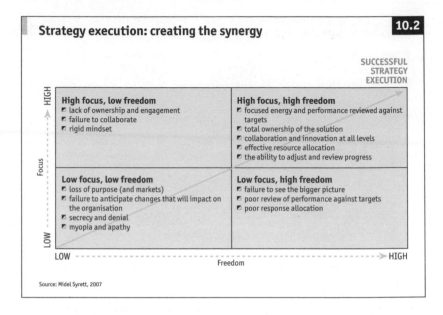

Strategy execution: creating the synergy `10.2`

SUCCESSFUL
STRATEGY
EXECUTION

High focus, low freedom
- lack of ownership and engagement
- failure to collaborate
- rigid mindset

High focus, high freedom
- focused energy and performance reviewed against targets
- total ownership of the solution
- collaboration and innovation at all levels
- effective resource allocation
- the ability to adjust and review progress

Low focus, low freedom
- loss of purpose (and markets)
- failure to anticipate changes that will impact on the organisation
- secrecy and denial
- myopia and apathy

Low focus, high freedom
- failure to see the bigger picture
- poor review of performance against targets
- poor response allocation

HIGH / LOW — Focus

LOW — Freedom — HIGH

Source: Midel Syrett, 2007

necessary collaboration and ability to adapt – which produce the resilience to face and overcome an almost constant state of external uncertainty.

Effective change management: a virtuous spiral

Each stage of the pathway shown in Figure 10.1, connected with the right leadership skills, contributes to a virtuous upward spiral that will enable an organisation to anticipate and respond to uncertainty and change on a self-sustaining basis (see Figure 10.3).

The nine milestones on the spiral, each representing a crucial stage of the process, are as follows:

- **Anticipate** the causes and implications of the change.
- **Assess** the organisation's ability to respond.
- **Determine** a strategy that will both respond to the immediate implications of the change and develop the organisation's change management capability.
- **Engage** the workforce by the right combination of communication, consultation and organisational response.
- **Support** the strategy through the right combination of dedicated milestones and performance measurements, training and learning opportunities and reward and recognition.

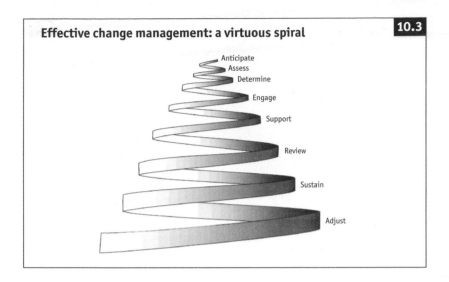

Effective change management: a virtuous spiral `10.3`

- Anticipate
- Assess
- Determine
- Engage
- Support
- Review
- Sustain
- Adjust

- ◪ **Review** progress regularly.
- ◪ **Sustain** the process by managing the pace of the change and introducing new challenges and goals.
- ◪ **Adjust** your thinking and your strategy in line with changing events and organisational feedback.
- ◪ **Anticipate** the causes and implications of the next round of change and thus re-embark on a continuous self-reinforcing process of response and adaptation.

Ineffective change management: a vicious spiral

By contrast, organisational psychologists such as Rosabeth Moss Kanter and learning experts such as Chris Argyris suggest that a failure to anticipate change or adequately prepare an organisation to respond to it leads to a vicious downward spiral of decline (see Figure 10.4 overleaf). If left unchecked, this leads inexorably towards financial collapse and the business failing.

The milestones of decline on this spiral, each of which leads to the next, are as follows:

- ◪ **Failure** to anticipate the nature and implication of change early enough to enable an organisation to respond.
- ◪ **Loss** of markets, status and/or key contracts.
- ◪ **Cutbacks** in resources and jobs.

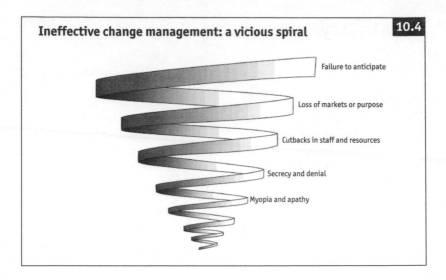

Ineffective change management: a vicious spiral `10.4`

- Failure to anticipate
- Loss of markets or purpose
- Cutbacks in staff and resources
- Secrecy and denial
- Myopia and apathy

- ◪ **Secrecy and denial**, blame, isolation and avoidance among key workers.
- ◪ **Myopia and apathy** in the mindset of managers who either determine or inform the strategy of the organisation.
- ◪ **Failure** to anticipate the nature and implications of the next round of change, and so on.

Once caught in this spiral, it is hard to simply stop and reverse direction. "Organisational pathologies arise and reinforce each other in such a way that the company enters a kind of death spiral," Kanter concludes. Reversing the cycle, using her formula for success, requires a well-crafted combination of open dialogue, engendering respect, sparking collaboration and inspiring initiative of the kind described in Chapter 7.

Summary

1 Setting the scene

Earlier pioneers of corporate transformation such as Lord King of British Airways and Jack Welch of General Electric created a template for strategy execution that became business school gospel and still determines the actions of chief executives today. It is based on the following tenets:

- cutting costs and unnecessary spending;
- breaking down internal barriers;
- focusing all resources on the main strategic goal;
- motivating and empowering the workforce around these goals;
- boosting performance as a result.

But the simple fact is that for most companies this strategy does not always work. Most organisations featured in this book have visions that are remarkably similar and consistent with those of virtually all businesses since the mid-19th century. They are to:

- be first (or a leader) in their chosen markets;
- produce a significant return on capital, through organic growth or acquisition and/or by reducing costs or making more efficient use of their resources;
- be innovative and creative in their product development, service design and delivery and work practices; and increasingly
- be ethical, socially aware and environmentally responsible in the way they conduct their business.

Yet the strategies they adopt to bring about these simple and straightforward visions all proved hard to implement in the first instance, and even harder to sustain. The causes of this friction are described in Chapter 2.

2 Friction

Friction – the factors that derail even the best laid strategy – occurs for a number of reasons, including the following:

- The target audience for the strategy is not static. The workforce

turnover of a large organisation can be equivalent to the
population of a small town during a five-year change programme.
◼ The goalposts move. Politics (big and small), egos, personalities,
misunderstood intentions, turf wars, departmentalised thinking
and changing organisational circumstances all combine to change
priorities, pushing the strategy down blind alleys.
◼ Poor operational accountability is rife. Either the goals do not
reflect the mission or people are not held accountable against them.
◼ Necessary information is imperfect. It is not available, or it is not
clear, or it is processed and interpreted differently by different
people.
◼ Middle managers complicate things. The more intelligent and
better educated individuals are, the worse the problem becomes
because of their ability to rationalise attitudes.

Research by Harvard Business School academics suggests that everyday
decisions two or three layers down the management hierarchy create –
and destroy – many organisations' strategies. The most important lesson
is that if every member of staff is clear about what they have to achieve,
everyone can be left free to decide how they undertake the task. For
everyone to profit from this freedom, however, they have to be given the
right focus.

3 Focus

◼ Providing a well-defined focus for any strategic initiative –
supported by goals and performance indicators – is critical, both
to engage the whole organisation and to enable line managers to
allocate resources correctly.
◼ Clarity is essential. Business goals are often complex, but they
must be simply articulated. The tasks of each business unit need
to be broken down into easy-to-understand objectives. Senior
management teams need to brief those who report directly to
them, a process that is repeated throughout the organisation until
everyone understands what they are doing and why they have to
do it.
◼ Mission leadership, based on the command doctrines of NATO
armies, provides an effective means to achieve this. Companies
as diverse as Diageo, Pfizer and Wal-Mart have used mission
leadership to foster innovation, articulate goals and turn around
senior management teams.

The military command doctrine on which mission leadership is based has the following elements:

- A commander gives orders in a manner that makes sure his subordinates understand his intentions, their own missions, and the context of those missions.
- Subordinates are told what they must achieve and the reason it needs to be achieved.
- Subordinates are given the resources they need to carry out their missions.
- The commander uses the minimum control measures (so as not to limit the freedom of action of subordinates).
- Subordinates then decide (within their delegated freedom) how best to achieve their mission. Put more simply: "Tell me what to do, not how to do it."

4 Communication

- Corporate transformation can no longer be imposed on senior management's own terms. The responses initiated to deal with the crisis fuelling the change will themselves throw up more (and probably unexpected) issues to resolve.
- The journey is often more important than its end. Change is continuous and uncertainty endemic, so the adaptive skills and attitudes acquired by managers and other staff along the way are as critical to the future sustainability and resilience of the organisation as the specific goals they are working towards.
- Sustainable organisations are amoebic and work underground. Formal communication and consultative processes launched to support a major management initiative need to be accompanied by intense networking using below-the-surface channels – what networking expert Karen Stephenson calls *social network analysis*.

5 Behaviour

People's behaviour determines whether a strategy will succeed or not. Identifying and shaping this behaviour lies at the heart of any approach to strategy execution.

Central to this is identifying the behaviours that will most contribute to the effective execution of the main strategy goals. Building on the analysis undertaken by Deutsche Bank, these may include:

- the degree of willingness by the individual to perform beyond the usually expected level (engagement);
- the urge in the individual to remain part of the organisation (retention);
- the individual's emotional involvement with the organisation (identification).

Building on the research of Julian Birkinshaw of London Business School, make sure that there is an effective balance between the following:

- Stretch – how individuals are stimulated to push for high-quality results and are held accountable for them.
- Support – how individuals get the tools they need to perform.
- Space – how individuals gain the freedom they need to choose their own path.
- Boundaries – the specifications of clear limits beyond which individuals must not stray.

Senior executives should create coaching and support systems that instil:

- a unifying focus on the main goals or mission of the strategy;
- a focus on customers and competition;
- an emphasis on effective teamwork and individual initiative;
- clarity about how individuals see their own role in achieving the main goals or mission as well as the roles of their colleagues and collaborators;
- a culture of collaboration between individuals, teams, work units, suppliers and stakeholders.

6 Measurement

Defects and breakdowns in measurement and performance management can seriously undermine strategy. These include the following:

- Companies rarely track performance against long-term plans. Less than 15% of companies make it a regular practice to go back and compare results with the performance forecast for each business unit against the strategic results for previous years. As a result, senior managers cannot easily know whether the projections underlying their capital investment and portfolio strategy decisions are predictive of actual performance.

◪ Multiyear results rarely meet projections. When companies do track performance, it rarely matches projections. The consequence is year after year of underperformance relative to the original plan.

◪ Value is lost in translation. A combination of poor communications, misapplied resources, limited accountability and lack of information creates a gap between strategy and performance. Performance bottlenecks are frequently invisible to senior management.

◪ Gaps between strategy and performance foster a culture of underperformance. Unrealistic plans create the expectation that plans simply will not be fulfilled. As this expectation is turned into experience, it becomes the norm that performance commitments are not kept.

Senior executives should establish a centrally co-ordinating office of the chief executive to:

◪ chart how various business functions contribute to the cross-disciplinary goals of the strategy, often in the form of a strategy map;

◪ make sure that the performance of business units, specialist functions and external suppliers and providers is aligned to these goals;

◪ distil these goals into team-based and individual objectives and make sure that they are cascaded throughout the organisation without the central focus and alignment being lost or watered down;

◪ develop the right measures and milestones so that performance is appraised effectively against these goals;

◪ engage in constant liaison with all levels of the organisation to make sure that essential resources – in the form of money, technology and people – are allocated to the projects and objectives that really contribute to these goals and are not frittered away on local managers' pet schemes or poorly focused initiatives.

7 Leadership

The focus on execution and performance is less on the leader's role as chief expert and chief discoverer and more on that of chief facilitator.

But this task is no less important. The strategy needs to be painted in the right context, articulated in a way people will understand as authentic, channelled and focused effectively, and supported with the right resources. This involves:

- generating engagement and commitment to the required change;
- imposing focus and clarity, pinpointing priorities and making sure they are adhered to;
- allocating scant resources to make sure this takes place;
- fostering innovation by encouraging and supporting the ideas and moulding the working practices of everyone who works for the organisation;
- creating the right milestones of achievement by using measures that illustrate effectively how far the organisation has progressed;
- managing the pace of change, shifting gear upwards or downwards according to how much stress the organisation can bear;
- sustaining the process by constantly reassessing the organisation's internal needs and anticipating the likely onset of further change triggered by outside circumstances.

8 Change

- Technological discontinuities, regulatory upheavals, geopolitical shocks, abrupt shifts in consumer taste and the rise of non-traditional competitors have all undermined the execution of even the most carefully thought-through strategies because they are difficult spot in advance and often hit industries simultaneously rather than in easy-to-control single packets.
- As a result, a new management discipline is emerging – managing uncertainty – which informs and determines both best business practice in industry and new management concepts in postgraduate and/or MBA programmes.
- Change management is intrinsic to successful strategy execution. The goal is to create an organisation that is as efficient at renewal as it is at producing new products and services.
- Minimising the trauma of change – in terms of unexpected surprises, convulsive reorganisations and across-the-board layoffs – is an integral part of achieving this goal. This emphasis on resilience fits in well with the broader imperatives of risk management and sustainability that are likely to dominate business strategy in the early 21st century.

9 Innovation

The essence of successful strategy execution is that if people are clear about the main objectives they can be given maximum discretion to be innovative about how they achieve them.

- Individuals will not be willing to take risks if they think they will be blamed if something goes wrong. They will judge whether this is the case not by what managers say but by what they do. Calls for greater creativity need to be matched by policies and actions that recognise and celebrate successes and enable both staff and management to learn from failures.
- Rewarding individuals for their creative contributions is important because it demonstrates that the organisation recognises that these contributions are discretionary and given because the individual feels motivated and intellectually stimulated. An award is as important as a reward because it makes the individual feel valued rather than simply being paid to be creative.
- Line managers can stifle the creativity of their staff, whatever the overall philosophy of the organisation. They should be mandated to foster and support innovation by championing, advising and shaping the ideas of their staff rather than seeing this as a purely discretionary role.
- The style in which creative teamwork is undertaken is critical to its success. Free-thinking discussions and censure-free, rapid exchanges are two of the many common features of successful brainstorms.
- For this reason, the role of the team leader or project manager is pivotal. Team leaders/project managers will usually choose members of the group and determine the working style. They also act as the team's shield, protecting it from unrealistic expectations, and as its resource gatherer, negotiating for it the means to get the job done.
- Imaginative assessment techniques will be needed to judge which creative output from a variety of teams is worth backing and which needs to be abandoned. If possible, this system of assessment should make sure that the thinking and insights of projects deemed to be failures are nonetheless preserved and transferred.

10 Pathway

This chapter distils the lesson from those preceding it into a pathway that can be used to manage the execution of any strategy effectively. Successful strategy execution depends on two factors:

- A focus on the right strategic goals, led and championed by senior managers, that unites the organisation behind the strategy, determines the measures and milestones of success and makes sure that resources – financial, technological and human – are allocated effectively.
- The freedom granted to individuals, teams, suppliers and strategic partners to be creative in finding new and innovative ways of carrying out these goals.

The capabilities required by the organisation to respond effectively to the right leadership are that it should be:

- **transparent** – letting everyone see everyone else's real work and letting people filter and sort for themselves;
- **engaging** – aiming to actively engage and involve workers not only in implementing the strategy but also in shaping it;
- **collaborative** – building on trust between people in the organisation and between organisations;
- **disruptive (and deviant)** – flushing out the rebels who thrive on disruption and nonconformity, making them the organisation's best agents of change;
- **well-networked** – enabling a free flow of ideas between work units and allowing centres of best practice to emerge and share their work;
- **amoebic** – adapting and shifting in line with change below the surface.

Appendix
Strategy execution: the military provenance

Some of the most important concepts of modern business strategy execution have a military provenance. No better example exists than the theories underpinning mission leadership, highlighted in Chapter 3.

The first part of this Appendix is based on an interview with Stephen Bungay, a military historian and author of *The Most Dangerous Enemy* (an account of the Battle of Britain) and *Alamein*, who is a director of the Ashridge Strategic Management Centre and a former vice-president of The Boston Consulting Group. He is an expert on the concepts of mission command and how it is applied in both military and business organisations.

In the second part, Mark Hartigan illustrates how the concepts of mission command have been applied in recent campaigns, most notably Kosovo and Iraq. Formerly a lieutenant-colonel in the British army, Hartigan was commanding officer of the 1st Battalion The Royal Irish Regiment in Iraq. He was subsequently promoted to colonel and now works in industry in the Middle East.

Mission command: a historian's perspective
Stephen Bungay traces the origins of mission command to the shattering defeat of the Prussian army at the battles of Jena and Auerstadt in 1806 by Napoleon.

In the wake of their defeat, the Prussians initiated a half-century of soul-searching and concluded that, as Bungay puts it, the pre-Jena Prussian army was "a highly process-dominated organisation based on the kind of top-down Taylorian management principles that dominated hierarchical business corporations in the mid-20th century".

Napoleon's army, by contrast, was distinctly non-Taylorian. According to Bungay:

> *Napoleon expected his marshals to use their initiative and act without orders provided they kept in line with overall intentions. They did. The result was that the French army possessed an*

operational tempo which ran rings around the drill-oriented
Prussians.

The response eventually developed by the Prussian army in the mid-19th century – and inherited by its German successors in the 20th century – was an operational command concept called *Auftragstaktik.* Developed by Helmuth von Moltke, the Prussian chief of staff, prior to the wars of German unification between 1864 and 1872 in which the Prussians trounced their former French Napoleonic opponents, it was later implemented successfully by the German officer corps during the two world wars. *Auftragstaktik* fostered independence of mind and maximum subordinate initiative.

In the confusion and uncertainty of war, people who exercise their own judgment run the risk of getting things wrong. But if the army was to demonstrate the kind of innovation showed by the French forces during the Napoleonic wars that was considered to be a risk worth taking.

The important prerequisite, as von Moltke concluded and Bungay stresses, is that that those at every level of the organisation understand enough of the intentions of the higher command to enable it to achieve its goal. Bungay says:

> Auftragstaktik, *as championed by von Moltke, did not want*
> *to put a brake on initiative, but to steer it in the right direction.*
> *Discipline did not mean following orders but acting in*
> *accordance with intentions. The phrase "thinking obedience"*
> *began to appear. Distinctions were made between an "order"*
> *(Befehl) and a "task" or "mission" (Auftrag). People started to*
> *talk about "directives" (Weisungen) as an alternative to orders.*

Bungay highlights a memo by Jacob Meckel, a Prussian general, in 1877 as the best definition of what this means in practice. General Meckel wrote that a directive had two parts. The first was a description of the general situation and the commander's overall intention. The second was the specific task. Meckel stressed the need for clarity: "Experience suggests", he wrote, "that every order which can be misunderstood will be." Bungay says:

> As General Meckel describes it, the intention should convey
> absolute clarity of purpose by focusing on the essentials and
> leaving out everything else. The task should not be specified in

too much detail. Above all, the senior commander was not to tell his subordinate how he was to accomplish his task, as he would if he were to issue an order. The first part of the directive was to give the subordinate freedom to act within the boundaries set by the overall intention. The intention was binding. The task was not. A German officer's prime duty was to reason why.

Auftragstaktik, as developed by von Moltke, underpinned the most important German military successes of the 20th century, including the Battle of Tannenberg against the Tsarist Russians in 1914, General von Manstein's Kursk campaign against the Soviet armies in the spring of 1943 and Rommel's desert victories in North Africa in 1941 and 1942. A contributing factor to the ultimate German defeat, according to Bungay, was Hitler's contempt for its principles and his attempt to reverse its practice.

The lessons it teaches – principally about the way soldiers should be led, not managed – was adopted wholesale in the modern doctrine of mission command espoused by NATO armies during the cold war and by American and British forces in recent wars in the Gulf and in Asia. Bungay says:

Today, the operational manuals of organisations like the US Marine Corps or the British army all contain passages which could have been lifted from von Moltke's original writings. Mission command is part of official NATO doctrine. Something like it, though not necessarily with the same name, has long been practised by elite forces.

NATO has realised that something like it was not just a burdensome necessity given the flexibility it suddenly had to have, but actually turned regular army units into high-performance organisations. It was first applied on a large scale in the Gulf war of 1991. It has been used on peacekeeping and security operations such as Operation Palliser in Sierra Leone in 2000. It was last put to the test in Iraq in 2003.

The techniques of mission command continue to be refined. It affects recruiting, training, planning and control processes and how operations are conducted. But its core is the culture and values of an organisation and a specific philosophy of leadership. It crucially depends on factors which do not appear on the balance sheet of an organisation: the willingness of officers to accept responsibility; the readiness of their superiors to

> *back up their decisions; the tolerance of mistakes made in good faith.*
>
> *Designed for an external environment which is unpredictable and hostile, it builds on an internal environment which is predictable and supportive. At its heart is a network of trust binding people together up, down and across a hierarchy. Achieving and maintaining that requires constant work. It is under test every hour of every day.*

And in this sense, Bungay concludes, it is capable of being transferred into the strategy execution doctrine of modern businesses, which also require a culture of trust, collaboration and interdependence with their workforces in an external environment marked by unpredictable and self-sustaining change.

> *A non-linear environment demands stepped responses, frequent small adjustments rather than periodic massive changes. In a world in which "no plan survives first contact with the enemy", people low down in the organisation must be ready to take the initiative and adjust as they go.*
>
> *To be able to do so, they must understand the intentions behind the plan. To be willing to do so, they need to understand the constraints under which they are operating, how much freedom of action they have and be assured that the organisation wants them to use it. Overcoming friction means working hard at alignment and also practising adaptive decision-making.*
>
> *We do not need more systems, plans or controls. We need to bring together the ones we have. Mission leadership provides a missing link between plans and actions, desired outcomes and actual ones.*

Mission command: a soldier's perspective

In May 1999 I was deployed into Kosovo as part of the NATO force. Before our move into the country we were massed on its southern border in Macedonia and received orders for the next day. There were uncertainties as to the extent to which the Serbs were going to fight, the level of ethnic cleansing the Kosovo Liberation Army (KLA) were about to embark upon, the effect of all the bombing upon our ability to move freely and the number of mines and booby traps awaiting us.

As a result, the orders were more about our commander's intentions than any specifics. We left knowing exactly what was in his mind, what he saw as the key requirements in time and space and action. I flew in early the next day ahead of my troops, who were moving in their columns up the Decani defile into Kosovo. We landed on a road just outside a burning village (to be sure to avoid the mines) and I met up with other commanders to receive instructions.

There was little time for anything comprehensive and the situation was evolving by the minute. My boss drew a big circle on the map and told me to get there, take it on as mine, clear it of Serbs, subdue the KLA, prevent further killing and get aid to the needy. It covered 22 towns and villages including the KLA stronghold in the south. He attached to me some pioneers, some tanks and some engineers and it was to be two weeks before I saw him again, by which time he expected the job to be well on the way to completion and me to have operated in line with his overall intentions for the region.

Situations such as this are not uncommon in my line of work. The nature of conflict is complex and on operations a commander exercises command of his force in conditions of uncertainty, risk, violence, fear and anger. In such circumstances, the apparently easy is made difficult and we call the resulting effect "friction". What we have to do is make our people comfortable among this chaos, to accept it as inevitable, and use it to generate disorder in the minds of our enemies.

Command, leadership and management

These are closely related. Major General Julian Thompson, who commanded 3 Commando Brigade in the Falklands war, said that management applies to things and leadership applies to people. Command (in particular identifying what needs to be done and why) embraces both management activities (allocating the resources) and leadership (getting subordinates to achieve it).

On operations, many of the management functions are subsumed by control. You may feel that command in a military sense is a far cry from resource allocation, budgetary responsibilities and associated management techniques, but these are becoming critical considerations in a host of military activities. Anyone seeking high command in the armed forces is introduced to the idea at our staff college, and our graduates will tell you that in modern operations aspects of command such as leadership, decision-making and control are interrelated and are an essential part of our command system.

For a long time, there has been a debate in the British army about the requirement for command and staff procedures to be based on detail and tight control and the need for decentralisation. During the cold war, NATO armies relied on a general defence plan that was a prescriptive response to the threat of invasion by Warsaw Pact forces. It was hampered by the political necessity to defend forward (and so protect Germany) and led to command in detail, which took likely scenarios and prepared for set-piece responses.

By the 1980s, however, we were free to cast aside such constraints and the concept of what we know as the manoeuvrist approach was formally adopted. Many would argue that its origins began 200 years ago in Napoleon's defeat of the Prussians at Jena and Auerstadt in 1806. Before this, command had evolved into what has been called command by plan, which opted for comprehensiveness over dynamism. In essence, it relied on a checklist by which engagements were to be fought. Napoleon's victories forced the Prussians to re-examine their methods and the result was *Auftragstaktik* or mission command (see Stephen Bungay's analysis above).

Why was this development necessary? In the 19th century there was a rapid escalation in military developments. Greater weapon accuracy, range and lethality dispersed forces and so increased the battle space. Telegraph increased the speed and flow of communications; railways and mechanisation increased the speed and capacity for movement. In the 20th century, soldiers were able to fight as well at night as during the day. Existing command systems were overwhelmed by complexity and information overload, but *Auftragstaktik* allowed the force to embrace disorder and deal with the friction of war.

British army doctrine remains based on a series of principles that shape our thinking (the Principles of War) and on the concept of manoeuvre warfare that reflects this approach. In simple terms, the doctrine emphasises the achievement of a position of advantage through manoeuvre rather than attrition. Here, manoeuvre refers more to an attitude of mind than to movement. It seeks to avoid trials of strength by attacking the enemy's will to fight and to attack the enemy at its point of greatest weakness. This approach requires a flexible attitude of mind by commanders at all levels. It requires us to exploit enemy vulnerabilities while maximising our own strength.

Decision-making, intent and fulfilment

The British army's philosophy for command has three enduring tenets: timely decision-making, the importance of understanding a superior commander's intention and, by applying this to your own actions, a clear responsibility to fulfil that intention. The underlying requirement is the fundamental responsibility to act within the framework of the commander's intentions.

This philosophy is not new. In May 1940, the seizure of the Belgian fortress of Eban Emael was a crucial precursor to the launch of the German campaign in the west. Its capture would allow the Wehrmacht's rapid advance across the Meuse river and the defeat of the French. Yet the detailed planning and execution of this special and critical operation was entrusted to a junior officer in the paratroopers with just 77 soldiers at his disposal. The plan required the troops to be glider-borne to gain access to the fortress and things did not go well.

A young officer, First Lieutenant Rudolf Witzig, was forced to make an emergency landing 100km from the objective, near Cologne. His second in command, Staff Sergeant Meier, did a little better and force-landed some 60km from it. Meier commandeered two trucks and drove the distance, threading his way through the waiting tank divisions, to begin the attack. Young Witzig, meanwhile, found himself another plane to pull his glider, landed in the fortress and brought about its surrender.

Action, freedom and speed of execution

Mission command, the approach adopted by the British army, promotes such decentralised action, freedom and speed of execution. It has the following elements:

- A commander gives orders in a manner that ensures his subordinates understand his intentions, their own missions and the context of those missions.
- Subordinates are told the effect they are to achieve and the reason it needs to be achieved.
- Subordinates are given the resources they need to carry out their missions.
- The commander uses the minimum control measures (so as not to limit the freedom of action of subordinates).
- Subordinates then decide (within their delegated freedom) how best to achieve their mission. Put more simply, "tell me what to do, not how to do it".

The army operates within the spirit of mission command in everything it does. Its application is of course more easily demonstrated in the immediate demands of military operations, but we use it at home and abroad in peacetime management of soldiers in barracks, in training for war and in war. It rests, however, on a number of principles being fully understood, fostered and frequently practised.

Principles of mission command

Unity of effort. How do you devolve decision-making without losing it? Unity of effort provides a focus for separate but co-ordinated actions. The adoption of a main effort that subordinates must support is a means of providing this focus. Each span of command will identify one and its achievement will enhance the command's ability to play its part in the higher commander's purpose. Linked to this is the understanding of the intentions of not just our immediate superiors but also those two levels up. Thus on deployment to Iraq, I gave my battalion orders within the context of not just my boss but also his boss. When my immediate subordinates gave their orders, they did it in the context of my intentions and those of my boss, and so on.

Decentralisation. There is nothing new here. The trick is that decentralisation should apply not just to headquarters and the higher echelons of command but to all levels. It requires in the higher command a corresponding flexibility of mind, confidence in subordinates and the power to make its intentions clear through the force. The more fluid the circumstances the lower the decision level should be set.

Trust. To be able to decentralise our actions we must have trust. It is the cornerstone of leadership and command and like respect it must be earned. For mission command to function effectively, a superior needs to have the trust of his subordinates and also to have trust in them. Soldiers must feel that they can trust not only their immediate superiors but also the chain of command to the top.

Mutual understanding. This is the bedrock of this two-way trust and covers a host of things. Commanders must have an understanding of the issues and concerns facing their subordinates. A common approach to command based on professional understanding of doctrine, drills and procedures, including the language of command, is also essential.

A commander's intentions must be clear if subordinates are to understand what they are to achieve. The most infamous unclear order in British military history, which preceded and provoked the Charge of the Light Brigade and the Battle of Balaclava, illustrates this point:

*Lord Raglan wishes the cavalry to advance rapidly to the front
and try to prevent the enemy carrying away the guns.*

We use a process known as mission analysis to translate our command-er's intentions into concrete activity. It ensures a thorough evaluation of the context of the operation, the purpose of those one and two levels above, the tasks that have been specifically given and those that are merely implied, and the freedoms and constraints that govern our actions.

Timely and effective decision-making. This is the last principle of mission command. It requires a commander to make a timely decision in relation to the opponent's own decision-action process. You have to know if a decision is required and when it has to be taken and by whom. Decisions on key issues are the province of the commander and should not be delegated to the staff. Having made a decision, you remain respon-sible for the direction of future planning.

Conclusion

I hope I have been able to make clear that mission command is about clarity of thought and expression. It is more than just a command or lead-ership technique. It is a discipline and a state of mind that leaders and the led need to understand. It is not an excuse for leaders to abrogate their responsibility to monitor and mentor. The back-briefing process, whereby subordinates offer updates and seek advice, is also an important tool.

The discipline mission command demands is not necessarily a military discipline. It is more an intellectual discipline to keep to its principal tenets as described above. Responsibility rests with the leader, who must deliver the co-ordination required to ensure that the components of the organisa-tion are working to the same end. Failure of one part will result in the chaos of the battle space being given free reign.

If many of you believe that what I have said is nothing but straightfor-ward common sense, I would say that common sense does not necessarily make for common practice. The execution of ideas is what we are about. I have always believed that there is an embarrassment of simplicity in what we do. Success depends on our continuing ability to make simplicity out of the chaos and complexity of war.

Note. This article is based on a presentation by Mark Hartigan to a gathering of senior business executives.

References

Chapter 1

1 "The cash-register guy", *The Economist*, March 18th 2006.

Chapter 2

1 Syrett, M. and Kingston, K., "GE's Hungarian Light Switch", *Management Today*, April 1995.
2 Marakon, M.K. *et al.*, "Turning Strategy into Great Performance", *Harvard Business Review*, July 2005.
3 Bower, J.L. and Gilbert, C., "How Managers' Everyday Decisions Create – or Destroy – Your Company's Strategy", *Harvard Business Review*, February 2007.

Chapter 3

1 Gratton, L., *Hot Spots: Why Some Companies Buzz with Energy and Innovation – and Others Don't*, FT Prentice Hall, 2007.
2 Bower and Gilbert, op. cit.

Chapter 4

1 Hamel, G., *Leading the Revolution and Competing for the Future*, Harvard Business School Press, 2000.
2 Anderson, C., "Bright young things: a survey of the young", *The Economist*, December 23rd 2000.
3 Lammiman, J. and Syrett, M., *CoolSearch*, Capstone, 2004.
4 Hemp, P. and Stewart, T.A., "Leading Change When Business is Good (interview with Sam Palmisano)", *Harvard Business Review*, December 2004.
5 Stephenson, K., *The Quantum Theory of Trust*, FT Prentice Hall, 2006.
6 Kennedy, C., *Guide to the Management Gurus*, 5th edition, Random House, 2007.
7 Interview with author in Syrett, M., *World Class Change Management*, Business Intelligence, 2006.

Chapter 5

1 Fischer, H. and Mittorp, K.D., "How HR Measures Support Risk Management: The Deutsche Bank Example", *Human Resource Management*, Winter 2002.
2 Birkinshaw, J., "An even-handed response to an uncertain context", *Financial Times*, April 7th 2006.
3 Ibid.
4 Ibid.
5 Interview with author in *World Class Change Management*, op. cit.
6 Ibid.

Chapter 6

1 Kaplan, R.S. and Norton, D.P., *Alignment: Using the Balanced Scorecard to Create Corporate Synergies*, Harvard Business School Press, 2006.
2 Kennedy, op. cit.

Chapter 7

1 Pascale, R.T. and Stevens, J., "Your Company's Secret Agents", *Harvard Business Review*, May 2005.
2 Kanter, R.M., "Leadership and the Psychology of Turnarounds", *Harvard Business Review*, June 2003.
3 Garvin, D.A. and Roberto, M.A., "Change Through Persuasion", *Harvard Business Review*, February 2005.
4 Bower, J. and Gilbert, C. (eds), *From Resource Allocation to Strategy*, Oxford University Press, 2005.
5 Gratton, op. cit.
6 Heifetz, R. and Laurie, D., "The Work of Leadership", *Harvard Business Review*, January–February 1997.

Chapter 8

1 George, N., "Ericsson back from the brink", *Financial Times*, March 29th 2005.
2 Sull, D., "Difficult decisions for an uncertain world", *Financial Times*, March 17th 2006.
3 Wind, J. and Crook, C., *The Power of Impossible Thinking: Transfer the Business of Your Life and the Life of Your Business*, The Wharton Press Paperback Series, 2005.
4 Wind, J. and Crook, C., "Changing mental worlds in an uncontrollable world", *Financial Times*, March 17th 2006.

5   Barsoux, J. and Bottger, P., "Can we really master uncertainty?",
    Financial Times, March 17th 2006.
6   Goffee, R., and Jones, G., *Why Should Anyone Be Led by You?*, Harvard
    Business Press, 2006.
7   Heifetz and Laurie, op. cit.

Chapter 9

1   Hamel, G., "The Why, What, and How of Management Innovation",
    Harvard Business Review, February 2006.
2   Lee, F., "The Fear Factor", *Harvard Business Review*, January 2001.
3   Hansen, M. and Von Oetinger, B., "Introducing T-Shaped Managers:
    Knowledge Management's Next Generation", *Harvard Business
    Review*, March 2001.
4   Devine, M. and Hirsh, W., *Mergers and Acquisitions: Getting the People
    Bit Right*, Roffey Park Institute, 1998.
5   Interview with author in Syrett, M. and Lammiman, J., *Successful
    Innovation: How to Encourage and Shape Profitable Ideas*, The
    Economist Books, 2002.
6   Lammiman, J. and Syrett, M., *Entering Tiger Country: How Ideas are
    Shaped in Organizations*, Roffey Park Institute, 2000.
7   Ibid.
8   Syrett and Lammiman, *Successful Innovation*, op. cit.
9   Syrett, M. and Lammiman, J., "Happily Landed", *People Management*,
    September 28th 2000.
10 Penn, A. and Hillier, W., *The Social Potential of Buildings*, Bartlett
    School of Architecture and Planning, University College London,
    1992.
11 Syrett, M. and Hogg, C. (eds), *Frontiers of Leadership*, Blackwell, 1991.
12 Interview with author in *Successful Innovation*, op. cit.
13 Lammiman and Syrett, *Entering Tiger Country*, op. cit.
14 Keelin, T. and Sharpe, P., "How SmithKline Beecham Makes Better
    Resource-Allocation Decisions", *Harvard Business Review*, March–
    April 1998.
15 Kim, W. Chan and Mauborgne, R., "Value Innovation: The Strategic
    Logic of High Growth", *Harvard Business Review*, July/August 2004.
16 Pascale and Stevens, op. cit.
17 Evans, P. and Wolf, R., "Collaboration Rules", *Harvard Business
    Review*, July–August 2005.

Index

Page numbers in *italics* refer to Figures; those in **bold** type refer to Tables.